inches 1 2 3 4 5 6

NUMBER OF TOES	CLAWS	GENERAL SHAPE	OUTLINE
4	YES	☐	
4	NO	○ OR ▭	
4	RARE	Ⓕ Ⅱ	
4 OR 5	VARIES	Ⓕ Ⅱ	
5TH TOE MAY NOT SHOW	OCCASIONALLY	Ⓕ Ⅱ	
5TH TOE MAY NOT SHOW	OCCASIONALLY	○ OR ☐	
5	OCCASIONALLY	Ⓕ Ⅱ	
5	NO	Ⅱ	
2	DEW CLAWS	☐	

F = FRONT   H = HIND   ● = ROUND

COMMON GAITS	SHAPE OF PADS	PAGE NUMBER
		35
		41
		46
		50
		61
		81
		91
		OPOSSUM 95 SHREW 96
		97

█ = LONGER THAN WIDE   ▬ = WIDER THAN LONG

A Field Guide to
Mammal Tracking
in North America

James Halfpenny

illustrations by Elizabeth Biesiot

Johnson Books

BOULDER

© 1986 by James C. Halfpenny and Elizabeth A. Biesiot
Cover design by Trish Wilkinson

Second Edition
15 14 13 12 11 10 9

ISBN 0-933472-98-6
LCCCN 86-80167

Printed in the United States of America by
Johnson Printing Company
1880 South 57th Court
Boulder, Colorado 80301

To my parents for all their years of support and caring.

Jim

To my whole extended family.

Liz

Contents

Acknowledgements

Since 1967 when I took my first photographs of tracks, many individuals have shared in field experiences and helped gather the knowledge contained in this book. Others have loaned me their photographs, collections, or notes or in some other way contributed to my knowledge of tracking. I wish to express my thanks to my colleagues and companions: Dave Armstrong, Nancy Auerbach, Steve Bissell, Norm Bishop, Scot Burns, Denise Casey, Tim Clark, Willie Cunningham, Scot Elias, Bill Ervin, Louise (Richardson) Forest, Rusty Fuller, Howard Hash, Bob Hasenyager, Larry Higby, Tass Kelso, Kathy Ingraham, Nan Lederer, Chris Linville, Larry Marlow, Carron Meaney, Anna Moscichi, Dave Nead, Rick Richards, Bob Rozinski, Dave Slovisky, Roger Smith, Jay Stravers, Bruce Thompson, Betsy Webb, Olwen Williams, and Kathleen Zinnel. If I have missed thanking anyone, please accept my apologies.

I wish to thank John Emerick for his encouragement in the initial stages of producing this book. Margaret Murie also was instrumental in her understanding encouragement. Drawings were made of the foot from the otter skeleton associated by George Northrup. Wendy Stout drafted the gait patterns and scat graphs. Tom Schenck of Camren, Inc., took the color photographs of the scat.

Special thanks go to Claire Sward and George Brown for my early field days. Much of my early tracking experience was sharpened by lectures prepared and given as part of the National Outdoor Leadership School instructor training program; thanks to Paul Petzoldt. While a hunting guide and game processor in Wyoming, I received many opportunities to work with mammals and their sign; thanks to Win Condict and John Dunlap. I wish to thank all the students who have shared experiences with me while at the Aspen Center for Environmental Studies, Teton Science School, the Yellowstone Institute, and at other special courses. Many of my photographs were obtained while working for the Colorado Division of Wildlife and in Canyonlands National Park. I thank Dave Armstrong and Steve Bissell for these opportunities. During special tracking classes I gave for the Colorado Division of Wildlife and Yellowstone National Park naturalists, I benefitted from interactions with many individuals, including Norm Bishop, Chuck Loeffler, and Tom Lytle. Teton Science School supported the effort necessary to prepare the final manuscript by providing housing, working space, and access to the Murie Museum. I would like to thank Jeff Hardesty and Greg Zeigler for their help and support. The Denver Museum of Natural History and the University of Colorado Museum provided valuable access to reference collections.

Draft manuscripts were reviewed by Dave Armstrong (University of Colorado), Gene Ball (Yellowstone Library and Museum Association), Norm Bishop (Yellowstone National Park), Mel and Sharon Cundiff (University of Colorado), and Kathy Ingraham. George Robinson (Yellowstone National Park) and Patrick Smith (Grand Teton National Park) provided valuable advice. I wish to especially thank them for their comments and help. For any errors, however, I accept responsibility.

1. Introduction

Wild mammals are among the most elusive animals in the world. With birds it is possible to go to the field and see many in a day's excursion, but this is not so with mammals. Many are nocturnal and they try to avoid humans at all times. For most people, much of what they learn in the field about mammals must come from the stories that they read in tracks. But reading these stories takes learning, practice, and experience. And that is what this book is about:— *how to understand tracks, interpret clues*, and *read trails of wildlife*.

The function of most field guides ends with the identification of an object or an organism. This guide is designed to do much more. Its purpose is not simply to identify specific tracks but to allow the user to understand the actions and behaviors recorded in the tracks and recorded by other clues. This is a field guide to **tracking**, not just track identification. It is designed to help you develop skills in interpreting the information left by mammals and to give you, the tracker, a glimpse into the secret lives of wild mammals.

Excellent field guides to track identification exist. As an additional reference, I recommend Olaus Murie's *A Field Guide to Animal Tracks*, and certainly the works of Ernest Thompson Seton will also make valuable additions to your book shelves. Other references may be found in the bibliography at the end of this book. However, new guides, since the work of Murie, offer disappointingly little new information. I believe you will find this guide to tracking new and invigorating in its approach and contents.

A DETECTIVE GAME

Think of reading tracks and stories as a detective game. First, you should try to gather all the **clues** possible. The more clues found and analyzed, the more educated your guess can be. Avoid the pitfall of guessing too early. Don't make a decision on the basis of simply one track; too often you will be wrong.

The realm of **clues** is large and includes geographic location in North America, habitat, season, ground surface, tracks, scat, and other sign such as broken or gnawed branches and hair. More helpful than a single track is a long series of tracks. Mental images you form while looking at one track may change if you can mentally average a series. Notice that I placed four types of clues before tracks themselves—location, habitat, season, and ground surface. You might have overlooked these clues but they are very important for setting the stage for the tracking story. When working with my students I require them to identify the stage-setting clues first. Then they must find at least three clues about the tracks and if possible some other clues *before* identifying the mammal and its story.

THINK LIKE AN ANIMAL

Most important in becoming a **nature detective** is for you to learn to think like an animal, more specifically, like a wild mammal! If I may be anthropomorphic for a bit: what controls a mammal's thought process is its stomach or its hormones. If a coyote is not successful at hunting, it can't go home to a master who will feed it. Domestic dogs can, and reliance on the constant food source shows in their tracks, which have a tendency to be sloppy and certainly don't reflect stealth. During the rut, the mating instincts (the hormones) of the mammal may override considerations of food.

A first, and admittedly crude, dividing line can be drawn between those animals that are normally prey animals and those that are normally predators. Prey animals must fill their stomachs with vegetation while predators must fill their stomachs with meat. Doesn't it make sense then that cottontail tracks seldom wander far from cover and burrows and that coyote tracks visit each nook and cranny?

Once you know the natural history of the mammals you are working with, it is easier to think like them. Later in the book there is a section on reading stories in trails. It will help you develop the skill of thinking like a wild mammal.

GOALS

I designed this book as a *how-to-guide* to be taken to the fields. I hope that whether you are a beginner or an expert you will benefit from the experience and the ideas that I have included and that Liz has illustrated with her sharp eyes and skillful hands.

For fifteen years now, I have been teaching classes on tracking. The students through the years have increased my understanding of tracks and have helped to consolidate and sharpen my concepts. In this book, I have tried to express the knowledge and principles you need to be a tracker. I have tried to answer the questions that I hear most often from beginners and experts alike.

The chapter on reading stories is designed as a self-teaching unit.

Information in this book is based on photographic slides and field notes that I have collected since 1968 and on experience gained since I was a Boy Scout in 1959. I was able to fill in some gaps by using the Olaus Murie Collection housed at Teton Science School. I couldn't cover every species of North American mammal, but I have covered representative species from each major group. Where the mammals of a group are easy to observe (the deer family) or are unusually significant (the bear family), I have tried to include as many species as possible. I have paid particular attention to aspects not well covered in other recent books on tracking: gaits, reading track stories, and scat. I hope the information contained here will make this a worthy reference source as well as an excellent teaching manual.

However, the most important goals of this book are to increase your awareness and understanding of mammals and to further your enjoyment of the outdoors. Whether you are hunter or non-hunter, this guide should make all mammals, in all seasons, "Watchable Wildlife!" Your trips to our national forests and parks can be enlightening as you learn to see what the mammals have been doing.

If you are an observant tracker, you will even learn to see stories of mammals in large cities. You will find many supposedly wild mammals (rabbits, coyotes, raccoons, skunks) within your city or on its edges. The skill of studying "urban wildlife" is an important one. When possible, visit your parks and stream beds, especially after snowstorms. Look for burrows, look under the bridges, and look under the dense brush—there are mammals there.

Each time you see tracks, even in the city, stop and study them. Each and every exposure to tracks adds a bit of knowledge to your experience. As time goes by, you will find it easier to interpret tracks, patterns, and trails.

COMMON QUESTIONS

Is it hard to identify mammals and read stories in their tracks?

No. With a little reading and practice you can identify a large number of mammal species and read interesting stories in their trails.

Can you always correctly identify the mammal that left a track?

No. Even the best naturalists can't always make a correct identification. Sometimes there are not enough clues, sometimes the clues are too old, and sometimes the clues are too ambiguous. Don't believe the "outdoorsman" who tells you that he can always tell an elk track from a moose track or the track of a coyote from that of a dog. It simply isn't possible to positively identify tracks every time. You analyze all the available clues and make the best educated guess possible. With experience, you will be correct much of the time.

Where can I find mammals?

Mammals are nearly everywhere. Learn to look for their signs. Even your pets produce interesting signs that can teach you a lot about tracking. The signs of mammals found in unexpected places are particularly rewarding. For instance, I have found tracks of lynxes visiting construction camps in Colorado, and I made the first verification that pocket gophers live in Canyonlands National Park, Utah.

A WORD OF ADVICE

When you are tracking mammals, it is possible to approach them closely. Wild mammals may be dangerous when you come within their defense perimeter. Use good judgment and don't get too close. Also, it is not fair to the mammal to be harassed by your close encounter. Be considerate as a naturalist!

When collecting, never take more specimens than is necessary or than you can properly take care of. Never collect rare or endangered species. You can visit scientific museums to observe those specimens closely. Also be sure you know the rules for areas that you are visiting. Collecting is not allowed in most parks. You will have to substitute photographs and notes.

MAMMALS

The word "animal" is a general term referring to living creatures, including crustaceans, insects, fishes, reptiles, amphibians, birds, and mammals. Mammals are differentiated from the other animals by several characteristics including the presence of hair and of several kinds of glands. At least two of the sweat glands are modified into mammary glands. Many species of mammals exist in North America, and you need to know a little about how they are grouped or classified (the science of **taxonomy**), in order to understand the tracks and sign that they leave. Mammals within the same groups share many characteristics and exhibit similar behaviors.

TAXONOMY

Mammals are classified by a heirarchical system that shows the relationships among groups. The units of this system and an example of how the coyote would be classified are given on page 6.

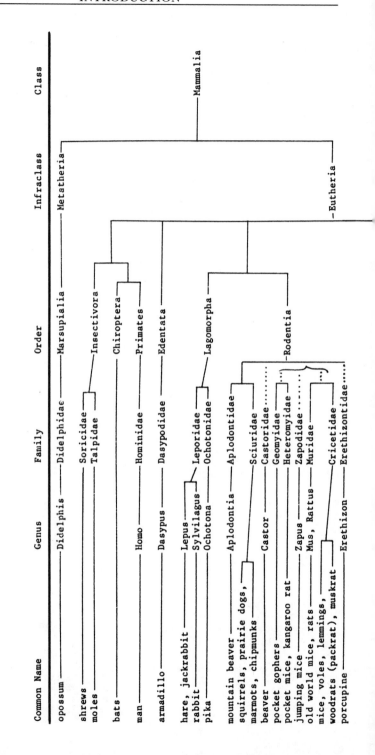

MAMMAL CLASSIFICATION

The family tree of *mammal classification* showing relationships between groups. For example, within the order Artiodactyla, muskox, mountain goats, and sheep are closely related to each other but more distant from bison. The family Bovidae is more closely related to the Antilocapridae than to the Cervidae. Exact relationships are not known within the order Rodentia and have been indicated by dotted lines.

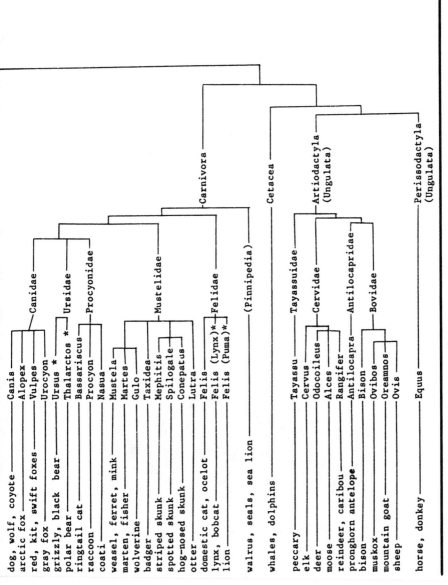

dog, wolf, coyote ——————— Canis
arctic fox ——————————————— Alopex
red, kit, swift foxes ——— Vulpes
gray fox ———————————————— Urocyon
grizzly, black bear ————— Ursus *
polar bear ————————————— Thalarctos *
ringtail cat ——————————— Bassariscus
raccoon ———————————————— Procyon
coati —————————————————— Nasua
weasel, ferret, mink ———— Mustela
marten, fisher ————————— Martes
wolverine —————————————— Gulo
badger ————————————————— Taxidea
striped skunk —————————— Mephitis
spotted skunk —————————— Spilogale
hog-nosed skunk ————————— Conepatus
otter —————————————————— Lutra
domestic cat, ocelot ———— Felis
lynx, bobcat ——————————— Felis (Lynx) *
lion ——————————————————— Felis (Puma) *

walrus, seals, sea lion ————————————

whales, dolphins ————————————————————

peccary ———————————————— Tayassu
elk ———————————————————— Cervus
deer ——————————————————— Odocoileus
moose —————————————————— Alces
reindeer, caribou —————— Rangifer
pronghorn antelope ————— Antilocapra
bison —————————————————— Bison
muskox ————————————————— Ovibos
mountain goat —————————— Oreamnos
sheep —————————————————— Ovis

horse, donkey —————————— Equus

Canidae

Ursidae *

Procyonidae

Mustelidae

Felidae *

(Pinnipedia)

Tayassuidae

Cervidae

Antilocapridae

Bovidae

Carnivora

Cetacea

Artiodactyla
(Ungulata)

Perissodactyla
(Ungulata)

* See index for more taxonomic information.
() Words in parentheses are informal taxonomic groupings.

Kingdom Animalia
Phylum Chordata
Class Mammalia
Order Carnivora
Family Canidae
Genus *Canis*
species *latrans*

The final two divisions, Genus and species, form the **binomen**, or two-part name, that characterizes each type of animal. The binomen is also known as the Latin name. The species is generally recognized as the level at which usual interbreeding stops. For example, three members of the Genus *Canis* are the coyote (*Canis latrans*), the domestic dog (*Canis familiaris*), and the wolf (*Canis lupus*). Under most non-human controlled situations these species rarely interbreed.

We can refer to mammals by either their common name or their scientific name. Scientific names have the advantage of being recognized worldwide, but they are not generally used by most people. In this text, I will refer to mammals by their common names; Latin names are listed in the index. The mammals have been organized by taxonomic group.

You will find it useful to know the main groupings of mammals: order, family, and genus. Within each level, common characteristics and behaviors are shared by grouped species. For instance, we expect all cats to have sharp claws and all weasels to have an odor. A taxonomic tree can be used to visualize the levels and relationships between groups.

The division at the family level is particularly helpful because most people know many of the families. Latin family names are changed to anglicized names by dropping the "ae" ending and adding an "s." For example, Canidae becomes canids, Felidae becomes felids, and Ursidae becomes ursids. I will occasionally use the anglicized version when referring to these groups.

The term ungulate has no official taxonomic meaning but is used to indicate both orders of hoofed animals, Perissodactyla (odd-toed mammals including horses) and Artiodactyla (even-toed including mammals). No native, wild perissodactyles currently exist in North America. Wild horses and burros are feral mammals introduced by European settlers. Therefore, I have not covered the order Perissodactyla in this book.

2. Using This Guide

I designed this guide to clearly explain how to track, to be easy for you to use, and to serve as a reference book in the field and at home. There are four basic parts:

1. a "how to" section, containing background information and techniques (Chapter 3 and 4)
2. details about mammal tracks by taxonomic group (Chapter 6)
3. a self-teaching section on reading track stories (Chapter 15)
4. an overview of studying scat (Chapter 16)

Before using this guide in the field, you should read Chapters 3 and 4 carefully. They explain many important aspects of using the guide and of tracking.

The area covered is North America

Area of North America covered by this book.

north of the Mexican–United States border. Some mammals just entering the U.S. from Central America, such as jaguarundi and ocelots are not included.

Two sets of graphic keys have been provided. These work like traditional dichotomous keys by separating choices into two categories at each step. However, they also allow you to see all characteristics and the end points at the same time. These keys are easy to use and should facilitate initial identifications. The keys will identify the general group to which a sample belongs. Further verification and identification to species should be based on the material in the main track section.

The key inside the front cover is to tracks and trails. The key inside the back cover is to scat. Both keys identify the specimen down to group level (family or order). The black bands in the track key align with bands on the appropriate pages. By flexing the pages, you can locate the section you want.

A second means of locating the desired taxonomic group is to refer to the **track formula** band at the bottom of each page in the main track section. The formulas are explained in Chapter 4. They may also serve as convenient memory aids for learning taxonomic groups.

Each section provides general information about the taxonomic group and species within the group. Drawings show key diagnostic points. Shadings and lines were added to emphasize important differences. We made a considerable effort to make the drawings as detailed and as accurate as possible. Dimensions and shapes of all drawings are to scale and correctly proportioned. The drawings represent the concept of averaging to arrive at the best image. However, each drawing, where appropriate, is based on a slide, actual specimen, and/or field notes. Location and size are noted on the drawing.

At the end of each section, a comparison page is provided. The text associated with this page explains differences to look for when you are trying to identify different members within a group. Common domestic species are included.

Liz has provided full-color pictures to illustrate some important behavioral situations that you can read in track stories. The color drawings will help you visualize the tracks and signs that would be present in these situations and will increase your ability to think like a mammal. Liz has adorned each species unit with drawings.

The section on reading track stories is designed as a self-teaching aid. Using a drawing from my field notes or experience, you will be asked to list as many clues as possible and then to identify the mammal and explain the story being told by the tracks. On the following page is a list of clues and the interpretation that I made in the field. Often you will be referred back to one of the full-color drawings to further clarify the story told by the tracks.

In the section about scat, I provide an update on the science of studying scat (**scatology**). Many new advances have been made in the last ten years, and much has been learned from bile analyses and detailed studies. We offer you information on how to identify mammal species from their scat, along with discussions on accuracy. Four pages of color photographs will help you identify scat. Diet analysis from scat is also discussed.

Liz and I hope that you enjoy this book and find it a worthwhile addition to your nature library and an important aid in the field. Take care of yourself and the environment, and have fun!

3. The Basics

The naturalist needs a framework of basic knowledge upon which interpretation of tracks and their stories can be built. This framework includes knowledge about mammalian structures and motion and the terminology necessary to convey that special knowledge. Knowing these finer points will enhance your understanding and appreciation. Below, I will cover the structure of the foot and leg, types of walking, terms and measurements, and mammal gaits.

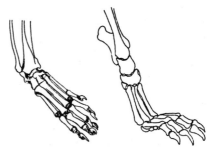
The hind foot of an otter and a coyote showing reduction of the fifth or smallest toe.

THE FOOT

The primitive mammalian foot consisted of five clawed toes, many bones, and probably a large number of supporting pads. Through evolutionary time there has been a tendency to reduce numbers of elements and, in the **cursorial** mammals (mammals evolved for speed, such as antelope), to streamline the form of the foot. Knowledge of the different types of foot anatomy will help you understand and interpret tracks and their stories.

Two major patterns are evident in mammals: the more complex foot observed in most mammalian species and the greatly reduced foot found in ungulates (see illustrations below). In the hind foot of the otter, five toes are present. Note that the first or inside toe has been reduced to only two **phalanges** (toe bones). In the front foot of the coyote, there has been further reduction of the inside toe until it has become **vestigial** (reduced until the organ, in the course of evolution, has lost most or all of its original function) and no longer even touches the ground. This toe is known as a **dew claw**. The first toe has been entirely lost on the hind foot. Examination of a pet dog will reveal these characteristics.

Ungulates show a more dramatic reduction in the number of bones. In artiodactyles, the weight is borne on the third and fourth digits only, resulting in a **cloven** (two-part) hoof. The first digit has been lost entirely, and the second and fourth digits are either greatly reduced (deer) or lost entirely (antelope). The third and fourth **metapodials** (bones above the toe bones) are fused into a single **cannon bone** to provide strength and streamlining. Horses, members of the perissodactyl order, show further reduction in that the weight is borne on the single third digit, resulting in a non-cloven hoof.

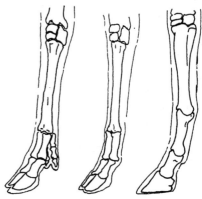
Leg bones of the elk, antelope, and horse show reduction in the number of bones.

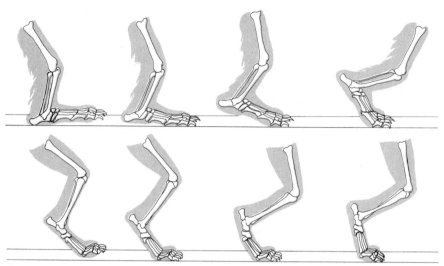

The heel of the plantigrade bear strikes the ground first and the whole foot is walked upon. The digitigrade coyote walks only on its toes.

These differences in limb structure are reflected in how mammals walk. Those that place their whole foot on the ground starting with the heel and rolling to the toes for the take-off are called **plantigrade**. We humans are an example of plantigrade mammals, as are bears. Mammals that walk on their toes, such as coyotes, are called **digitigrade**. The extreme specialization found in ungulates is often referred to as **unguligrade**, a form of digitigrady. In general, plantigrade mammals move slower than digitigrade mammals and spend less time trotting or galloping. (Additional information can be found in Ewer and Vaughan).

Pads on mammalian feet provide traction and absorb the shock of landing when the animal runs or jumps. The pad arrangements on the feet of the gray squirrel resemble the evolutionarily primitive situation. Each toe has a pad directly below the tip, the **toe pad**. Behind the toe pad is a group of **plantar** pads (also called **interdigital** or **intermediate** pads). Behind the plantar pads are one or two **metapodial** or **proximal** pads (called **metacarpal** pads on the fore feet and **metatarsal** pads on the hind feet). The proximal pads form the heel. The sole refers to the whole bottom of the foot.

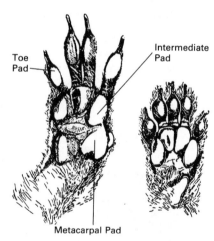

Names of the pads on the front (left) and hind feet of a gray squirrel from Michigan.

The inside plantar pad, known as the **pollical** pad on the fore foot and as the **hallucal** pad on the hind foot, is reduced or absent when the first digit has been lost through evolution, as in the front foot of the squirrel. Interdigital pads may fuse to form large pads as in the canids, and metacarpal and plantar pads may fuse to form larger pads as in the ursids.

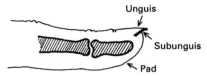

This cross section of the idealized digit shows the position of the claw and pad.

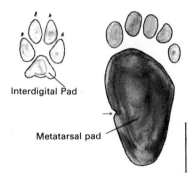

The interdigital pads join to form one pad in the dog print and the metatarsal pads join to form a large heel pad in the black bear print. Scale is 2 in (5 cm).

Claws are hardened material derived from hair. They are composed of two parts: The harder **unguis** (top) and the softer **subunguis** (bottom). These structures are directly homologous to the human fingernail. In humans, the ubunguis is the small amount of soft material found under the leading edge of the fingernail.

The cloven hoof of even-toed ungulates is derived from the third and fourth toes. The highly modified hoof consists of three parts: the **wall** (unguis), **sole** (subunguis), and **pad** (**frog** in horses). In clear tracks, all three parts can be identified.

The amount of space occupied by the pad within the wall is characteristic of different species. In elk the pad occupies a small space, but in the moose it takes up most of the room within the wall. Two dew claws are present in most ungulates, appearing as small hooves well up the leg. Dew claws are higher on the hind legs than on the front legs. Antelope do not have dew claws.

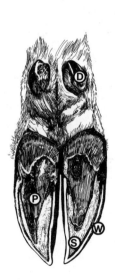

The pad (P), sole (S), dew claw (D), and wall (W) may be identified on elk and moose feet from Jackson Hole, Wyoming. The pad takes less space in the foot of an elk (right) than it does in the foot of a moose (two feet on left). Dew claws are higher on the hind legs (outside) than on the front legs.

MEASUREMENTS
AND TERMS

To help us understand and communicate the information we find in tracks and trails, we need to define our terms. The terminology that follows represents a workable system derived from experts in the field. However, when you read other natural history works, be aware that the authors may have used terms somewhat differently, and consistency between authors is rare. I don't wish to imply that these are the only usages of terms, but I want to provide a defined, working vocabulary for this book.

I use the words **print** and **track** synonymously to refer to the imprint left on the ground by a single foot. A **trail** consists of a line of prints and sign left by one animal (some authors prefer to call this a track). **Pattern** refers to the spatial arrangement of the tracks. We **trail** an animal that is moving in front of us, but **tracking** is the science of following a line of prints and signs that were left sometime in the past. Tracking includes the use of all clues, not just foot prints. **Stalking** is the art of moving up on an animal without the animal being aware of our approach.

I encourage you to take as many measurements as possible to further your knowledge of tracking. It is best to draw the tracks and trail and to fill in the measurements on your drawing. I suggest that you use graph paper and draw to scale when possible. Stretching a piece of string or marking a line indicating the direction of travel will be helpful. This line should lie in the center of the trail pattern. Measurements are illustrated below.

For individual footprints, measure the **length** and **width**. The length of the print is measured from the leading edge of a toe pad print to the trailing point of the print. Claws are not included because their length may change with the mammal's activities; for instance, bears digging underground bulbs in the spring will have shorter

claws than during August when they are feeding on berries. If claws are present, you should also record the distance the claws extend beyond the toe imprints. **Width** is measured at the broadest point of the print.

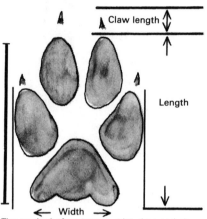

The method of measuring print sizes and claw length is shown on the coyote print. Scale is 2 inches (5 cm).

The proximal pad often does not show in a print. Therefore, be careful to indicate the ending point for your measurement.

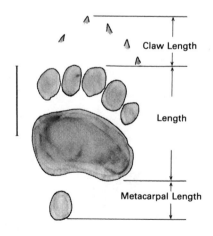

The method of measuring the metacarpal or proximal pad is shown on the grizzly print. Scale is 4 in (10 cm).

For ungulate tracks, measure the **interhoof distance**. It is also helpful to

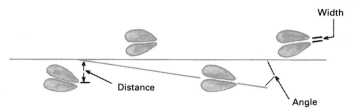

When measuring a deer trail, establish the line of travel as a reference.

record the **angle** that prints make to the direction of travel. This may be estimated, or if scale drawings have been made, measured later with a protractor. The distance that the front of the print deviates from the line of travel may be substituted for an angle measurement.

Stride is the distance from where one footprint appears in a trail to the next point that a footprint made by the same foot appears. This measurement must be recorded from the same point on the first print to the same point on the next print. I suggest that the trailing edge be used. The stride, as defined, includes two full walking **steps**. Other authors have used stride to refer to one step. After many years, I now prefer this definition because the stride during a normal walk then equals the body length of the mammal from its hips to shoulders and is directly indicative of the animal's size.

Stride

The method of measuring stride shown on a bobcat trail.

Straddle is measured perpendicular to the line of travel at the widest point of a trail or group pattern. The straddle is measured to include the width of the tracks. To aid in the measurement of the width, you can draw a line between the outside edges of two prints that represent a stride, e.g. two left hind feet. Then measure to the outside edge on the print in between, in this case the right hind print.

Measurement of the stride gives a di-

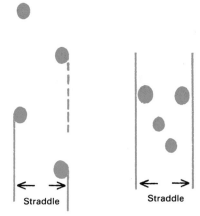

Straddle   Straddle

The method of measuring staddle is shown on a coyote (left) and rabbit trail.

rect comparison of speed, no matter what gait a mammal uses; longer strides indicate faster travel. As speed increases, the stride will increase and the straddle decrease. Rough differences in straddle exist between types of gaits: the straddle decreases in width from walk to trot and then to gallop.

When they walk, mammals leave a pattern consisting of two parallel rows of prints. However, when they speed up, they leave other characteristic patterns indicative of the type of gait being used. We call these patterns **groups**. The group pattern is measured from the leading end of the pattern to the trailing end of the same pattern so as to include prints from all four feet. **Intergroup** measurements are made from the leading point of one pattern to the trailing point on the next pattern. Note in the illustration how this measurement differs from stride.

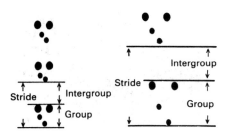

Trails of a rabbit showing how to measure stride, group, and intergroup distance. A longer stride is evident in the trail of the faster moving rabbit on the right.

Track Formula

As a memory aid, I have developed a shorthand method of recording track information. The **track formula** indicates common characteristics within a group. A typical formula would appear as follows:

f5(4) H5(4) co

This formula is indicative of the bear family and reads: the front print usually shows five toes but occasionally only four will register; the lowercase "f" indicates that the front print is smaller than the hind print (capital "H"); the hind print usually shows five toes but may occasionally show only four; claws often show.

Note that formulas refer to what registers in the print on the ground, not to actual anatomy. For instance, the dog family has a fifth toe on the fore foot, but this very rarely shows in a print. Therefore, the formula would be F4. A lowercase "f" or "h" indicates the smaller pair of feet of the mammal. Several abbreviations refer to claws:

C   = claws usually show
co   = claws often show
cr   = claws rarely show
     = a formula without a "c" indicates that the claws don't show

Formulas are shown at the bottom of each page of the tracking section. It is possible to identify animals once you have interpreted the clues in reference to their track formula. By thumbing the pages, the correct group can be quickly located.

Front and Hind Tracks

A brief word about **fore** and **hind** feet. In many orders of mammals the fore feet are slightly larger than the hind. This is to be expected since the fore feet must carry the burden of the relatively heavy neck and head cantilevered at an angle in front of the rest of the body. For mammals with larger fore feet, the front prints are generally larger. But this may not be obvious.

There is also a tendency for the front toes or hooves to splay more, especially when the mammal is moving fast or on soft ground. These characteristics will help you distinguish feet. However, when the hind foot registers directly on top of the front print, it usually obliterates the front print.

GAITS AND TRACK PATTERNS

You can identify mammals from their tracks and read the stories told in their trails easily if you understand how mammals move. The relationship between prints shows the type of mammal, the speed it was moving, something about its personality, and even its emotions at the time it left the prints. You may be able to identify a mammal's tracks at a great distance because of the pattern of the tracks. This may be accomplished without studying a single print. However, as a tracker you need an understanding of gaits to interpret the trail.

A **gait** is a coordinated pattern of movements used by an animal when it moves. The simplest gait is a walk; some other gaits include trot and gallop. Each gait leaves a characteristic signature in the print patterns on the trail.

Below, I present a classification of gaits and information on how to interpret trails left by mammals using those gaits. The classification represents the first system showing the relationship of gaits to track patterns for all the gaits of North American mammals.

CLASSIFICATION OF TRACK PATTERNS

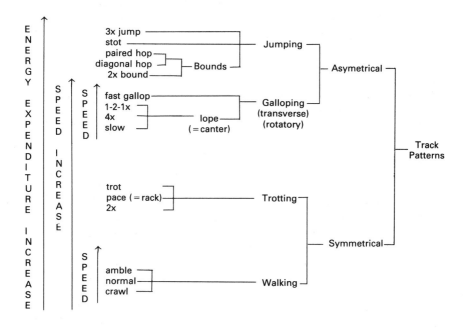

A tree showing **Classification of Track Patterns** left by various gaits. Although there are many gait patterns recognized by the use of slow motion cameras, I list only 15 track patterns. Patterns may grade into each other and absolute separation is not always possible. General trends of increasing speed and energy expenditure are shown on the left. Within the galloping and walking groups, the patterns are arranged by increasing speed and energy expenditure. Terms with a number, such as 2x trot and 1-2-1x lope, are read two-by trot and one-two-one-by lope. Terms such as 2x refer to the arrangement of feet within each group track pattern as observed on the ground. Other common names of gaits are shown in parentheses. Two types of gallop patterns, transverse and rotatory, may be observed depending on which foot, right or left, leads. See text for further explanations.

As I developed this classification, I was influenced by the work of several authors and naturalists: Bang, Bullock, Ewer, Hildebrand, and Muybridge. In addition, you can find accurate records of trail patterns in Murie, Smith, and the many works of Seton.

Naturalists have used terms referring to the gaits of mammals inconsistently, incorrectly, and often without adequate definition. For example, the terms "lope" and "run" have been used rather indiscriminately. I hope the following section will clarify terminology, facilitate your natural history observations, and increase your enjoyment of tracking.

The terms **run** or **running** are too general and have no accepted definition when referring to gaits. Different authors have referred to trots, gallops, and lopes as running. The average person understands running in terms of human or bipedal motion where running is merely a faster extension of the motion of walking. However, that situation is neither analogous nor translatable into the motions of quadrupeds.

Gaits of North American mammals and the resulting track patterns may be divided into four main types: walk, trot, gallop, and jump. We can group the gaits into those that are symmetrical—the walk and trot—and those that are not—the gallop and jump. In symmetrical gaits, the interval between footfalls is evenly spaced, and track patterns are symmetrical for the right and left sides of the trail. In asymmetrical gaits, there is an uneven spacing of footfalls and the right half of the track pattern differs from the left. Gradations exist between gaits, and some movements by a mammal may not be easily classified, although most will fit into these categories. Transitions between gaits may defy classification, and movements made on uneven surfaces or while turning will be hard to classify.

We have illustrated track patterns with stylized drawings in this chapter. As you read the descriptions, refer often to the illustrations, for they will help you get a feeling for the patterns left by different gaits. It will take some studying for you to understand the patterns and what they are telling you about the movements and emotions of mammals.

The illustrations are all drawn to the same scale so that relative changes in straddle, stride, group, and intergroup dimensions are apparent. Direction is indicated by the triangle and all patterns start with a right fore foot. Variations in trails, reflecting changes in gait, are shown as the trail pattern progresses.

Trails are symmetrical, and they may be either right-handed or left-handed. Therefore, for each illustrated pattern, a mirror image pattern exists.

Study the illustrations well, for they contain a vast amount of information.

Walk

All terrestrial mammals **walk** at least occasionally, although for many, such as the rabbit, walking is not their most common gait. When walking, a mammal moves each foot independently of the others. During a slow walk (**crawl**), three or even four feet may be on the ground at one time. However, at a fast walk, known as an **amble**, a maximum of two feet will be on the ground at one time. At no time during a walk are all four feet off the ground. Walking is a slow means of movement and is relatively energy efficient.

The trail left by any mammal when walking shows two parallel rows of alternating, evenly-spaced prints. The stride is short and the straddle is wide. Direct register of the hind foot on top of the front foot occurs in animals moving cautiously, such as a stalking carnivore, or in deep snow. Direct register is commonly observed in the dog family. However, much of the time the hind foot will slightly overstep the front foot. Raccoons have a peculiar walking gait in which the hind print is beside the diagonal front print.

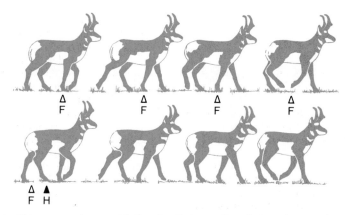

Pronghorn utilizing a normal **symmetrical walk** with two or three feet on the ground at all times. An observer has the impression that the hind feet are treading on the front feet. Note that the hind print registers in front of the front print on the same side. F is the position of the front track and H is the position of the hind track (after Bullock).

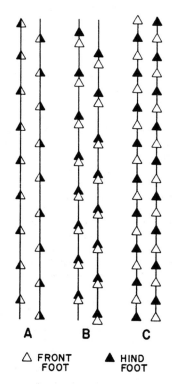

Walking Track Patterns
A. Hind foot registers on front print.
B. Hind foot slightly overstepping front foot.
C. Walking pattern of raccoon.

△ FRONT FOOT   ▲ HIND FOOT

Trot

Trotting, a faster mode of locomotion, is energy efficient relative to the speed obtained by the mammal. The animal appears to be gliding. Many mammals, such as elk, are able to trot for extended periods of time. While trotting, the two diagonal feet move simultaneously. Each front foot moves at the same time as the diagonal hind foot. As each diagonal pair of legs leaves the surface, there is a period of flotation during which all four feet are off the ground.

The trail left by a trotting mammal shows two parallel rows of alternating, evenly-spaced prints. You can tell this trail from a walking trail by its narrower straddle and a greater stride. Generally in a trot, the hind foot will register in front of the fore foot. As the trotting mammal increases speed, the overstep by the hind foot increases, as does the distance between pairs of prints.

Members of the dog family, especially the fox, occasionally move with an interesting variation of the trot. Their bodies are held at an angle to the direction of travel so that all front prints show on one side while the hind prints show on the other. Hind prints usually register slightly in front of the fore prints. I call this pattern the 2x trot as it leaves

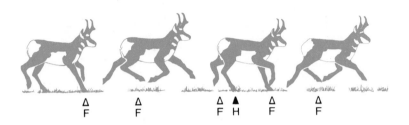

$\underset{F}{\triangle}$ $\underset{F}{\triangle}$ $\underset{F}{\triangle}$ $\underset{H}{\blacktriangle}$ $\underset{F}{\triangle}$ $\underset{F}{\triangle}$

Pronghorn utilizing a symmetrical **trot**. An observer receives the impression that two feet come together while two feet are apart. Note that in this fast trot, the hind foot print is well in front of the front print on the same side. F is the position of the front track. H is the position of the hind track.

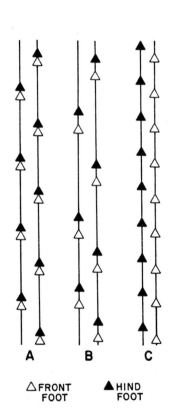

A   B   C

△ **FRONT**   ▲ **HIND**
  FOOT   **FOOT**

Trotting Track Patterns
A. A slow trot that appears similar to a walk but with a longer stride.
B. A faster trot with the hind foot overstepping the front print.
C. A 2x trotting pattern often seen in the dog family. Hind prints are all on one side of the line of travel.

Fox at side trot.

The movements of a fox when using 2x trot with front prints registering on one side of the line of travel and hind feet registering on the other side.

two prints at an angle to the direction of travel.

Another trotting gait in which two feet move simultaneously is the **pace** (also known as the **rack**). During the pace, lateral feet, one fore and one hind, move together. This is a very rough movement and is seldom used by North American mammals. However, it is the normal gait of camels. Trotting mammals, such as members of the deer family, do not pace naturally. Wider-bodied animals might occasionally pace, and pacing has been observed rarely in cats and dogs. However, I do not agree with Brown who believes that wide-bodied animals use the pace as their normal slowest means of moving. I believe that the pace is the exception rather than the rule in nature.

The trail left by a pacing animal looks similar to the walk of the raccoon. However, careful study of Muybridge's photographs of a raccoon walking shows that the pattern with the fore foot opposite the diagonal hind foot is indeed a product of a walking gait.

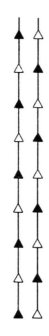

△ FRONT   ▲ HIND
   FOOT   FOOT

Pace Track Pattern
The stride length separates the pace pattern from the walking pattern of a raccoon.

Gallop

The **gallop**, which is the fastest of gaits, leaves an asymmetrical track pattern. Energy expenditures are high, and most of the time the gallop is not continued for long periods. The diagnostic characteristic of a gallop is a major airborne phase when the animal takes off from the fore legs. Gallops with only one airborne phase are known as **lopes** or **canters**. During particularly fast gallops, there may be a second airborne phase when the animal takes off from the hind feet. During a gallop, the straddle is reduced considerably, and prints lie nearly on a line in the direction of travel. Gallops may grade into jumps, and you can not always differentiate between the two gaits.

Two types of gallops are known: the **transverse** (or **cross**) and the **rotatory** (or **rota**). The difference depends on which hind foot leads by striking the ground first. We show the sequence of footfalls in the transverse gallop as a cross and the sequence of footfalls in the rotatory gallop as a circle. Of course, either pattern may progress from a left or a right direction. Mammals may use either pattern, but the cross gallop is commonly found in horses, buffalo, and cats. The rota gallop is found in the antelope, and in the deer and dog families.

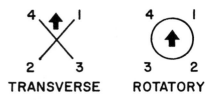

Order of footfalls in transverse and rotatory gallops.

We have illustrated five patterns characteristic of the cross gallop. As speed increases, the overstep of the hind feet increases until both hind feet register ahead of the fore feet. This stretching of the gallop pattern results in the different patterns we observe in trails.

The first three patterns represent relatively slow gallops. We call these **lopes**. The 4x lope (or gallop) is common and is characteristic of the dog family. The 1-2-1x lope is common in the weasel family.

The term **lope** has been used interchangeably to describe the 2x trot and the 4x and 1-2-1x gallops. However, the trot is a symmetrical gait, whereas the gallop is asymmetrical. Therefore, lope should not be used to describe both types of gait. The slower galloping gaits are designated lopes.

In the minds of most people, the lope is an energy-efficient gait that can be used to cover great distances. While trots are considered energy efficient, I

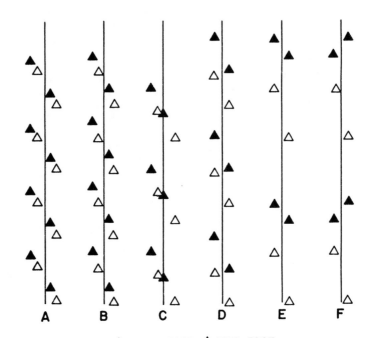

△ FRONT FOOT ▲ HIND FOOT

Gallop Track Patterns

A. Slow lope   D. Faster gallop
B. 4x lope   E. Still faster gallop
C. 1-2-1x lope   F. Rotatory gallop

A through E are transverse gallops.
Notice that as the speed increases from A to E, the overstep of the hind prints increases. Straddle is narrower in faster gallops.

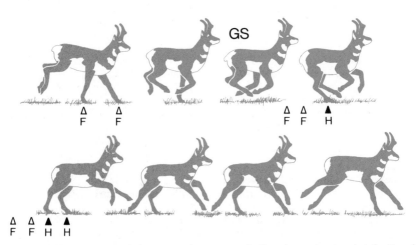

Pronghorn utilizing an asymmetrical **transverse lope**, a type of gallop where only one period of gathered suspension (marked GS above) occurs. The take-off for the suspended period is from the front feet. In the transverse lope the right, or diagonal, fore foot strikes the ground after the left hind foot. An observer has the impression of all four feet coming together and then the front feet being separated from the hind feet. F is the position of the front track and H is the position of the hind track.

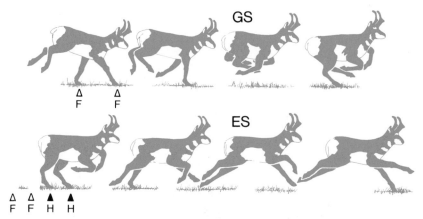

GS

ES

Pronghorn antelope utilizing an asymmetrical **rotatory gallop**. In the full gallop there are two periods of suspension: a gathered suspension where the animal takes off from the front feet (GS above) and an extended suspension where it takes off from the hind feet (ES above). In the rotatory gallop the left or lateral fore foot strikes the ground after the left hind foot. The observer has the impression of all four feet coming together and then the front feet being separated from the hind feet. F is the position of the front track and H is the position of the hind track.

believe that the slower gallops (lopes) may be more energy efficient than the faster trots. This is probably true for those mammals adapted through evolution to use the lope as a principal method of moving.

Only one rota gallop pattern has been illustrated. As in the transverse gallop, there will be similar changes in the relative position of the hind prints to the front prints as speed increases. The most common and characteristic gallop within the dog family leaves a "C-shaped" (or reverse "C-shaped") pattern. This pattern is left by a rota gallop when the lead of the hind feet has changed. The pattern is also common in the deer family.

Jump

The **jump** is an energy consuming and strenuous gait and, although similar to the gallop, it is slower. The jump is characterized by one flotation phase when the animal takes off from the hind feet or all four feet. A second flotation phase may occur when the animal takes off from the fore feet. The most prominent phase is initiated by the hind legs, and landing is on the fore legs. The fore

legs then leave the ground briefly before the hind legs land in preparation for another jump. Hind legs usually land laterally and to the front of the fore legs.

Five jumping track patterns are common: diagonal front feet hop, paired front feet hop, 2x bound, 3x jump, and the stot. Hopping, characteristic of the rodents and lagomorphs, and bounding, characteristic of weasels can be grouped under the common term bounding. The stot is used by the deer family. Jumping is employed by mammals in deep snow, when suddenly frightened, to clear obstacles or to pounce on prey.

The diagonal front feet hop is characteristic of those animals that spend most of their time on the ground (for example, ground squirrels, chipmunks, and rabbits). The hind prints are nearly perpendicular to the line of travel, and the front prints are at an angle to the direction of travel. Front feet may exchange the lead.

The paired front feet hop is characteristic of those animals that spend much of their time in trees, such as tree squirrels. Both the hind and front prints are nearly perpendicular to the line of travel. In some situations, the front prints will form pairs with the hind prints. At other times the front and hind

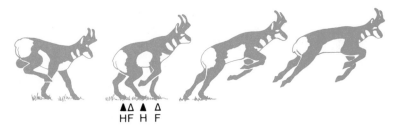

△△ ▲ △
HF H F

Pronghorn antelope **jumping**. The gathered phase is very short with all four prints close together and the takeoff from the hind feet F is the position of the front track and H is the position of the hind track.

prints will be so close together that they form one indistinguishable pattern on each side. These 2x jump patterns perpendicular to the line of travel are indicative of tree squirrels.

The 3x jump pattern is used by many mammals for making quick jumps or when only a few jumps are made in the row. The pattern is particularly common in the cat family. When the alternating fore feet leave the ground, one print is covered by a landing hind foot, leaving only three visible prints.

The 2x bound is characteristic of the weasel family. After both fore feet leave the ground the hind feet land on the positions that the fore feet occupied. In contrast with other jump patterns, there is a definite tendency for the two resulting prints to be at an angle to the line of direction. One fore foot and one hind foot lie on each side of the line of travel. The 2x bound may be transitional between a lope and a jump.

A stotting pattern results from a mammal jumping from all four legs simultaneously. This gait is common in deer, especially during the rutting season when it may serve as a mating ritual. The stot is also a response when suddenly frightened. The track pattern shows evenly spaced prints. Often little horizontal movement occurs between successive stots.

Interpreting Gait Patterns

The use of a particular gait reflects the task of the animal at the time, since most mammals have the ability to use any gait. An animal that is not in a hurry, say a grazing animal, will take its time and walk. An animal needing to cover a long distance but in no hurry

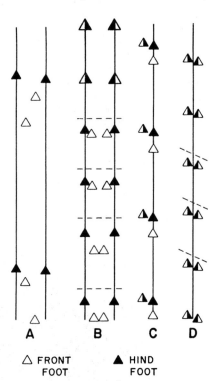

A   B   C   D

△ FRONT   ▲ HIND
   FOOT   FOOT

Jumping Track Patterns
A. Diagonal front foot hop. Notice the switching of the lead front foot.
B. Paired front hop on 2X hop, characteristic of tree dwelling mammals. All patterns are perpendicular to the line of travel.
C. A 3x jumping pattern with one front print hidden under a hind print.
D. The 2x bound of the weasel family. The track pattern is at an angle to the line of travel.

When the rabbit **hops**, the hind feet overstep the front feet leaving a short group pattern with the hind prints in front of the front print. The intergroup distance is relatively long.

will use a trot. This might include an antelope moving across its range or a scavenger seeking to explore large areas. A lope, the most energy-efficient of the gallops, might also be used. An animal in a hurry will gallop for short distances; startled animals jump. A carnivore may jump or gallop at the end of the stalk. A particularly short walking pattern followed by a jump may indicate stalking. However, remember that the characteristic gait of the hoppers (rabbits and rodents) is a bound. Hoppers show changes in attitude and speed by elongating or shortening within the group hop pattern.

Changes in gait represent changes in the mammal's attitude. This change may be as simple as slowing down to rest or speeding up at the sight of a predator. Look for these changes in the lengths of group patterns. Sudden turns are always worth investigating as they may reflect major changes in attitude.

The foot print provides a standard of comparison for the mammal you are trailing. Speed may be judged by comparing the stride and straddle to the standard—the foot print length. Strides, which are short compared to the foot print length, indicate a mammal that is moving slowly. Strides that are many times the length of a foot print indicate speed.

4. Tracking Techniques

Telling someone how to track is analogous to telling someone how to play the piano. I might tell you everything about how to play, but to become a concert pianist, you would have to sit down and practice. The same is true of tracking. In this section, I will provide the "how to," but you will have to get out and practice. I wish, as a teacher, that I could be there to point out the clues, but I can't. Therefore, I will take this opportunity to explain as much as I can and trust that you will practice becoming a tracker.

SEARCH IMAGE

The most important skill of tracking is learning to see. Although this may sound like a basic skill that all people have, it is not. Time and again, a skilled naturalist will be able to look at the ground and see things that others miss. The naturalist will be able to piece a few visible parts together into a whole story. Why? The naturalist has developed a **search image** in the mind and has also developed a "discriminating eye." A search image is a mental image you can cue in on. Have you ever sorted objects—for instance coins? As the sorting progressed, your speed increased. The increase was due to cueing in on different types of coins. The men-

tal construct, we call the search image, may be a complex picture consisting of several basic track shapes and patterns.

Try to develop your search image and the skill of knowing what to look for by practicing on a small area. This should be in an area where you know animals, even pets, have been, and it should be about one square yard (meter) in size. Sit down and spend fifteen minutes or more just looking at the ground for tracks and track patterns. In this exercise, don't neglect bird or other tracks. It is important to recognize these other tracks so you can differentiate them from mammal tracks. Sketch the block of ground and the patterns it contains.

You can develop a discriminating eye by learning to recognize tracks from different perspectives. As you look at your mini-plot, move around from side to side. Look straight down. Look from a low angle. Look into the sun and shade the study area. Study parts of a single track so that you will recognize a print when you see only portions of it. Also look at the bigger picture. When looking at a single track, look at the area two or three inches (5-8 cm) around it. Then step back and look at the whole picture; study the complete trail and identify the different gaits you see.

POSITIVE VERIFICATION

Positive reinforcement is a great aid to the learning process. I highly recommend it for trackers. When you see a mammal, even a pet, carefully go over the area where it was. Look for its tracks, scat, and sign. Compare these clues to the behavior and action you observed. These positively verified clues are important additions to your lifelong collection of experience. When you are collecting, try to include as many verified specimens or photographs as you can.

EQUIPMENT AND PRESERVING TRACKS

Several methods have been used to record tracks, including drawings, photographs, and casts. Of these, I favor drawing and photography over casts. Plaster for casts is heavy, and the final products are bulky and fragile to store. In the rush of the modern world, it is hard to take the time to buy plaster and then to carry it on every trip. However, casts do make nice projects for classes, and students and other naturalists like something that they can actually hold in their hands. Wood putty has been used with success to make casts.

Recently we have been experimenting with foam insulation. Moderate success was obtained using foam available in spray cans. The nozzle of the can is placed under a 4x6-in (10x15-cm) or larger file card. As the foam is sprayed under the card, pressure is placed on the card to force the foam into all corners of the track. Field notes may be written on the card after the cast dries. The resulting casts are light-weight, and rough edges may be trimmed with a knife. A can of spray foam is lightweight, and water does not have to be available. There are many brands, and you may have to experiment to find the most workable one for your situation.

Take along a notepad and a camera on your trips. You need little skill to make sketches that will be valuable to you later. With modern films, it is possible to easily record many of the tracks and trails observed in the wilderness. The higher speed films, such as Ektachrome 100 or 200, are recommended because tracks in the dirt are often very dark, and color rendition is not critical. If a photo flash is not available, a flashlight will often add enough light to make it possible to take pictures under extreme conditions. Sometimes a flash can be used to bring out the relief in the print. When shooting with a flash, shoot at an angle to the track, not straight down. If you can take the flash off the camera, hold it so the track is crosslighted to provide better contrast. Whenever you take pictures be sure to include a scale. A six-inch ruler is easy to carry, but anything of known size can be used. Place it as close to the track as possible to limit distortion from parallax. When possible shoot straight down on the print. A tripod will help you get good depth of field under limited light conditions as well as avoid the single greatest cause of poor pictures—camera movement.

Several other items may be of use. A pocket tape measure or a folding carpenter's ruler can be used to measure longer sections of trail and to provide a center line for your photographs. Some lumber stores now have plastic folding carpenter's rulers that will not warp due to water or wet mud. Ziploc™ bags are a boon to the modern field naturalist because they provide a secure means of collecting field items. However, you must take moist items out of bags upon returning from the field and dry them. You can make small envelopes from newspapers for drying; the newsprint is porous. Film cans from 35 mm film are also excellent containers for field collections. A package of 3x5-in (7.4x13-cm) file cards and pencil will allow you to make notes to be placed in collection bags. I recommend pencils over pens as many inks will run when wet. I have found the Pentel™ mechanical pencil with thumb-advancable lead to be outstanding. The pencil carries its own supply of lead, and new pieces may be advanced without opening the storage compartment. Colored pencils are nice for sketching scat or scenes.

Although I am an avid advocate of written field notes, I have found pocket microcassette recorders to be an important addition to my field gear. They will allow you to quickly collect data when conditions do not lend themselves to taking field notes. The tapes can later be transcribed to notes and even saved. You must keep the microcassette inside your coat when it is cold out.

FIELD NOTES

Field notes are of critical importance to amateur and professional naturalists. As each year goes by, details become fuzzy and are lost from our memories. Field notes therefore increase in importance with the years.

Well-kept field notes also help you gain the respect of other naturalists. For instance, a good field notebook increases your credibility when reporting a rare sighting to a national park or animal preserve.

For a field notebook, I recommend a three-ring binder using readily available 8½ x 11-in (22 x 28-cm) loose-leaf paper. This allows you to take out pages for files. Pages can also be added as needed.

There are three parts to the field notebook: the journal, the species account, and the catalog. The **journal** is similar to a diary. In it, you record all the general notes of your trip such as dates, times, who was with you, locations, weather, distances between points, ecological communities, and general observations.

The **species account** consists of a separate page for each species. At the top of the page write the name of the species. Whenever you learn something about a species record it on that page. For instance, record in the journal that a coyote was observed on the trip, but in the species account list all the details about the animal's behavior. With each item in the species account you should write supporting information, including date, time, location, and weather. Completed species account pages should be filed at home in a separate folder for each species.

The **catalog** is where you record any collections that you make. Start each entry with a unique number and attach that number to the specimen so it cannot become separated. Write on the specimen with indelible ink if possible, otherwise tie a tag to it. Also record supporting information including date, time, and location where the specimen was collected.

Jospeh Grinnell developed the formats for taking good field notes. You will find further readings on this important subject in articles by Halfpenny, Hall, and Herman.

To use with the established system, I have developed a **track account** page. This page is part of the species account; file it with the corresponding species accounts. I have included a blank form.

Check points are listed to remind you of the type of information that should be obtained. Try to fill in each category of information every time you record tracks. Take as many different measurements as possible and record several replications of each for averaging. Record only one species per sheet.

You might want to develop a blank format sheet and photocopy it. The use of graph paper is suggested for doing accurate scale drawings. I have included a page of my notes so you may see what information is gathered.

STAGE SETTING

When you find a set of tracks, think for a minute about the stage on which your story is about to unfold. **Geographic location** may limit the possible species with which you are working. **Habitat** also serves to limit possible species. To interpret the location and habitat, you will need to increase your familiarity with the natural history of mammals through experience, classes, and readings at home.

The **season** of the year will also provide clues. Look for foxes living in dens in the spring. However, they will be only

Name_____ Date_____ Species_____

Location_____

Habitat_____ Surface_____

Check Points: Right vs Left, Front vs Hind, Tracks vs Trails,
              Types of gaits, Relative Size, Other Clues

Sketch Tracks and Trails:

Measurements (units are _____):   (Make additional drawings on back)

No.	Front L	Front W	Hind L	Hind W	Stride	Straddle	Group	Inter Group	Claw L	Metacarpal Length	Interhoof Distance	Angle

Name *Jim Halfpenny* Date *Nov. 17/85* Species *Domestic Dog*

Location *South of Lot #95, Mapleton Trailer Park, Boulder, Co*

Habitat *City* Surface *Concrete Sidewalk*

Check Points: Right vs Left, Front vs Hind, Tracks vs Trails, Types of gaits, Relative Size, Other Clues

Sketch Tracks and Trails:

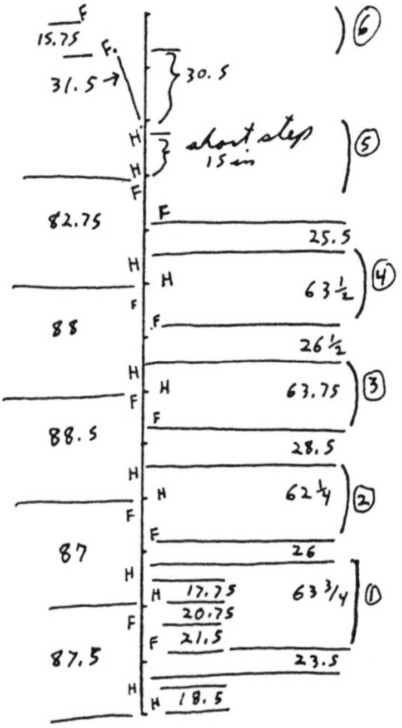

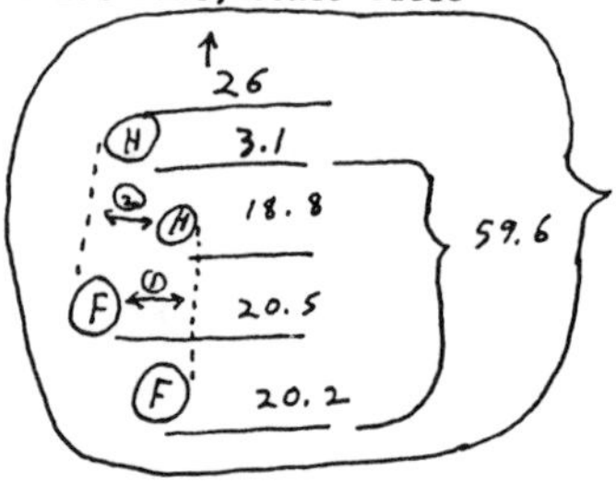

Transverse Gallop Pattern

Front to Front 21.5, 19.75, 20, 19.5 / x̄ = 20.2
Front to Hind 20.75, 21, 20.25, 20 / x̄ = 20.5
Hind to Hind 18.5, 17.75, 19, 19, 19.75 / x̄ = 18.8
These measurements are by groups 1 to 5 as numbered on left.

note: First straddle measurement (① in gallop pattern above) is always larger than second (② above). Measurements below.

Measurements (units are *inches*): (Make additional drawings on back)
Prints on Back

No.	Front L	Front W	Hind L	Hind W	Stride	Straddle	Group	Inter Group	Claw L	Metacarpal Length	Interhoof Distance	Angle
1R	3 3/4	2 3/4	3 1/4	2 5/8	87.5	4 3/4 / 4		23.5				
1L	3 1/2	3	3 1/4	2 5/8			63 3/4					
2R	3 1/2	3	3	2 1/2	87	5 1/8 / 4		26				
2L	3 1/8	2 7/8	3	2 1/4			62 1/4					
3R	3	3	–	–	88.5	4 3/4 / 3 1/2		28.5				
3L	2 7/8	3	3	2 1/4			63 3/4					
4R	3	2 7/8	3 1/4	2 1/2	88	4 3/4 / 3 3/4		26.5				
4L	3	3	3 1/4	2 1/4			63 1/2					
5R	3 1/4	3 3/8	2 7/8	2 1/2	82.75			25.5	F = 1/4			
5L	3 1/2	3 1/8	3 1/8	2 5/8					H = 1/2			
x̄					87.75 n = 4		63.2	26				

the females giving birth and raising their young litters. Mothers will be accompanied by young during the summer. Many ungulates migrate to winter ranges in the fall. Males of the deer family remove the velvet covering on their newly-grown antlers in the fall and destroy saplings in the process.

Determine what the **surface** was when the mammal made the tracks. Time will have elapsed since the tracks were made, the surface may have changed, dirt may have dried out, or slush may have frozen. The surface will affect the size of the tracks. Tracks are smaller on hard surfaces and larger on soft surfaces. Follow the trail under a tree and then into the open. The surface may change dramatically in these two situations. In snow, it is often possible to obtain a clear print under a tree but not in the open. Muds with differing contents of clay will dry at different rates. Actively growing plants spring back to position quicker than those that have, stopped growing for the year.

AVERAGING

When you are following a trail, I suggest you use a process I call **averaging**. First, take all the measurements of the prints and the trail that you can. From your measurements, calculate average dimensions.

Next, step back and look at several tracks, or better yet, follow the trail for a distance. While following the trail, develop a mental picture that averages the shapes of the prints. As you develop the picture, consider what the surface under the tracks was at the time the tracks were left, and from the gait estimate how fast the mammal was moving. The difference can be dramatic. A fast-moving animal may leave larger, deeper tracks. Also consider whether the animal's foot has slipped or if it was going uphill or downhill. When an animal is traveling uphill, its stride will be shorter. It may be helpful at this point to draw a picture of the average shape.

The type of surface changes the size of a print. A bobcat's print appears small in the dust, yet large in the mud. Scale is 2 in (5 cm).

The averaged print will be a better representation of the mammal's track than individual prints. Once you know the average print, including size and shape, then you are better able to judge what mammal you are tracking.

RELATIVE SIZE

I do not emphasize learning dimensions of mammal tracks. Too often I have observed the use of cited dimensions as the absolute criteria defining species identification. While well-intentioned, the size criterion fails to consider the variation in the genetic pool of mammals, the variation over geographic distances, and the variation caused by different surfaces. Too much variation exists among species for a single criterion to be very effective. Any single cutoff point will discriminate against one species or another. For further illustration of the problem of variation, see the discussion and illustrations in the section on scat.

Instead of absolute measurements, I emphasize learning to judge **relative size** within taxonomic groups. For example, compare members of the dog family. The fox is the smallest member of the family, and its dainty tracks leave a delicate, almost cat-like impression. In contrast, the wolf is the largest member of the family, and the robustness of the animal is immediately apparent in the print. Using the concept of relative size, the "robustness" or "delicateness" of a track, will tell you the size of the mammal that made the track. Even a small wolf track will be robust.

Judging relative size will also increase your awareness and help you think like a wild mammal.

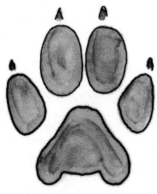

Relative size comparisons of fox, coyote, and wolf.

The skill of judging relative size can be learned at home, even in the city. Observe pet cats and dogs and compare their body size with their feet and the size of prints they leave. Compare the robustness of the print with the physique of the pet.

I am not implying that actual dimensions are not important but that you can benefit by learning to work from relative judgements rather than trying to memorize all the absolute dimensions. When appropriate, dimensions are listed with drawings and are presented on the comparison page for each taxonomic group. I suggest that you will benefit more by not memorizing these dimensions but only using them as a check and as another clue for making educated guesses. The practice of taking measurements when prints are recorded will enhance your ability to judge relative size and to relate that judgement to absolute sizes.

CLAWS

The appearance of claws in tracks can be confusing. Ideally, the claws will show as unattached depressions in front of each toe. The depressions may be either simple round holes or wedge-shaped indentations. However, many times the imprint of the claws will be continuous with the toes. The resulting impression is of a relatively bigger and pointed toe pad. Learn to recognize pointed impressions left by claws and to distinguish these from the toe pads. The toe pads may show a rounded point. Study closely the drawing of the coyote print below.

Claws in a print register in various manners. Different visual impressions appear in this wolverine print including the lack of a claw on one toe.

IDENTIFICATION OF SEXES

Many times when following a trail you can, with careful observation, verify the sex of the animal being tracked. Size, posture during urination, blood, and social behavior are important indicators.

The female of most North American mammal species tends to be smaller than the male. This is particularly true within the weasel family, where the **sexual dimorphism** is rather dramatic. Remember, though, that the tracks of a small female long-tailed weasel will look like the tracks of a large male short-tailed weasel. Tracks will reflect the size difference but are not absolute indicators of sex. Don't believe the person who says you can identify the sex of elk or deer by size alone. Size is an excellent clue, but only a clue, as there are large bucks and small bucks.

Within the dog and cat families and ungulate group, posture during **urination** can be an excellent clue. When males are urinating, the stream tends to be directed forward of a well-placed pair of hind legs. Therefore, the **urine** stain will appear well in front of the hind legs. For females, the urine stain

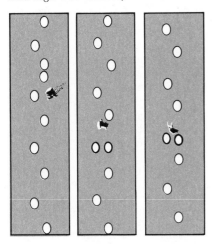

The position of the urine stain identifies the male coyote (left) and the buck deer (center). Notice the far forward position of the stain in reference to the hind feet of the buck. The stain from the female (on the right) is close to the hind feet.

appears only slightly in front of the hind legs.

Male canines also lift their hind leg to **scent mark** an object by urination. The exception is wolves, where both the dominant male and female mark by leg lifts, and subdominants of both sexes do not utilize a **leg-lift** marking (see plate 1). Cats also mark territories by expelling urine directly backwards onto an object. Urine has a distinctive odor, both to the mammals that leave it and to us. Use your nose as well as your eyes.

While tracking coyotes and bobcats, I have observed blood droplets on the snow and in association with urine stains. Coyotes and wolves are seasonally **monestrous**, showing one period of **"heat"** per year. Blood may flow from the vulva before **estrus**. I presume this is true of bobcats and of at least some of the other carnivores. The presence of blood is probably a good indicator of sex if found in association with urine. Other bits of blood on a mammal trail might come from an injury, especially to the foot. Check for the origin of the blood by noting its position in reference to urine and tracks.

Social organization tends to keep females associated with young animals. A large set of tracks with one or two smaller sets may represent a female with her young. This may be of great importance to you, for instance in grizzly country. It is not wise to surprise a grizzly with her young! Ungulates often form separate male and female herds. The male and female young are found with the adult females during the late spring and summer and to a lesser extent during the breeding season.

OTHER MAMMAL SIGN

Many types of mammal sign exist, ranging from bones to limb-chewing to scat. I will discuss scat extensively in a separate chapter. Here, I would merely like to alert you to the realm of clues that you may obtain from other types of sign.

Chewings on branches or tree trunks are among the most easily observed sign. First, note the location of the chew: high in the tree (porcupine), about 3 in (8 cm) up the trunk (voles), about 18 in (45 cm) up the trunk (possibly beaver), under a low branch but done by a mammal on the ground (porcupine), or shoulder height (ungulate). Relative size of the debarked area may help you distinguish squirrel chews from porcupine. When investigating chewings, note the width of individual teeth and the direction that the teeth moved through the bark. Relative tooth width helps distinguish mouse from squirrel and squirrel from porcupine chews. Ungulates debark trees by raking their lower incisors (they do not have upper incisors) up or at a slight angle to the tree trunk. Porcupine and beaver chew at great angles to the trunk (see plate 2).

Antler trees or **rubs** are those trees used by the ungulates to scrape the velvet from their newly grown antlers (see color plate 3). During the process, much of the bark is scraped from the tree. The edges of the bark appear very frayed and do not show the clean cut of chewed bark. Most rubbing activity occurs in August but may vary in different geographic areas. Usually deer, elk, and moose will select a small sapling or group of saplings. These may be bent over double and occasionally snap while the animal is scraping. Less often, the ungulates use larger diameter trees. In Yellowstone, Norm Bishop (Assistant Chief of Interpretation, Yellowstone Park) showed me larger trees scraped by bison. Certainly the bison, mammals with horns, are not trying to remove velvet, but they do scrape the bark from trees. Norm also observed a bison horn the bark from a lodgepole pine and eat a three-foot strip as we would eat spaghetti.

Marking trees are used by members of the bear and cat families. The trees, marked by scenting, rubbing, clawing, and chewing, probably hold much more significance for the mammals than we humans perceive. A bobcat clawing a tree may be merely sharpening its claws, but I doubt it. Whether we can perceive the true meaning of these trees or not, they are important clues about the life of the mammals.

Bears work on trees near their commonly used trails. They will stretch as high as possible to claw the sides of the trees or simply to rub their backs all over the trunk, breaking off small limbs (see plate 4). This rubbing may be to alleviate an itch, but I suspect that it is related more to the habit of carnivores rolling in scat and remains of animals and is a form of scent marking.

Bears, especially grizzlies, will occasionally debark most of a tree trunk. Evidently, this is to get at the sweet sap of the **cambium** or inner bark layer. The presence of long, fine, kinky bear hair (as opposed to the coarse undulating hair of the ungulates) verifies identification. Claw marks can be separated from antler fraying by looking closely for indications of four or five claws starting high and being raked down the tree. With antlers, some of the motion is upward, and seldom do you find an even spacing of rips that would indicate claws. Herrero provides an excellent discussion of marking trees used by grizzly bears.

Small **twigs** are often eaten by rodents and lagomorphs. Size of tooth marks and the amount of chewing necessary to completely sever the end of a branch are important clues. Rabbits, jackrabbits, and hares are often able to completely sever a small branch in one bite, whereas a vole takes several bites (see plate 5). Winter chewings may be higher on the tree than you expect because small mammals may have been working from a platform of snow or from within the snowpack. You can tell the browsing of moose and other ungulates by the jagged edges left on the branches. Ungulates lack upper incisors, so they mash and tear off small twigs instead of cutting them off. When heavy snow is on their range, elk and deer will eat the bark and lower branches of conifers and other trees. Heavy use causes a **browse line** and is known as **highlining.**

The width of tooth marks on a twig indicates the size of the guilty mammal. A small rodent chewed the twig on the left and a rabbit chewed the twig on the right.

Grazing activity of ungulates can be detected by observing blades of grass for squared-off ends that have started to brown. Trails can be seen crossing a meadow (when tracks are not visible) by the displacement of grass blades. This is particularly evident if dew or frost is present in the early morning.

JUDGING THE AGE OF TRACKS

As trackers, we generally want to know how much time has elapsed since a mammal passed. To know this, you must look at a track and judge its **age**. The ability to age a track is a skill that can be learned. There are two phases that you must practice. The first is construction of a test pit and the second I call the step test.

Test pits can be constructed anywhere, including your back yard. Select an area of exposed soil that is not going to be disturbed for a few days. Start at one end by making a single footprint; note the appearance of the fresh track. I believe that it is more educational to use actual prints than to make a mark on the ground. Taking notes or photographs will help later. One hour later add a second track at the side of the

first. Then add a track at four, eight, sixteen, and twenty-four hours. Each time you add a track analyze the effects of aging on your known-age prints, and note what factors may have changed their appearance: rain, frost, wind, etc.

To gain experience, construct test pits in other surface materials such as grass, mud, snow, and gravel. Also construct pits so the study period will overlap with major climatic events such as a rain, a nightly freeze-thaw cycle, or a wind storm.

The **step test** is performed when you are actually looking at a track. Simply step next to the print you are observing (the reason for practicing on your own footprints earlier). Evaluate the difference in the appearance of the two tracks. One process, gravity, ages all tracks. As time goes by, the edges lose their sharpness and start to fall into the print. How much decay has occurred due to gravity? From your experience with the test pit, make an initial estimate of age.

Next think back over the last two hours, the last eight hours, and the last day or two. Recall what the weather has been. Has it rained? Snowed? Has the wind blown? Has there been a freeze-thaw cycle? Did the sun shine? Has the soil dried out? When did these events occur? Tracks left early in the morning may show fresh damp soil thrown up. Pock marks may be present from rain, or fine dust may have been blown in. Was the morning dew or frost disturbed by the mammal? Tracks made in the snow last night may show refrozen water-ice in the bottoms, newly formed ice crystals, or hoar crystals on the surface indicating the tracks were made before last evening. The edges of the snow may show cornice formation due to the wind. Revise your estimate based on answers to these questions.

Look for other clues that may help you age the trail. If the vegetation was bent by the passing mammal, has it regained its former position? Remove soil and scat from the vegetation where it has fallen. Is the vegetation from under the scat still as fresh appearing as the vegetation beside it? If so, the tracks are fresh. Can you still detect moisture in the scat? Is it still steaming? With these last clues, make your final estimate of the age of the track.

FOLLOWING A TRAIL

When you follow a series of tracks, you can do several things to help yourself visualize and understand the trail. Walk beside the trail so you do not disturb the tracks. Mark those tracks you might like to return to later for photographs or detailed measurements.

Try to track into the sun if possible. If not, occasionally stop and turn to face the sun as you look at the tracks. This procedure may emphasize relief in the tracks. This is a good time for photographs.

Frequently shift your gaze from the tracks directly at your feet to some distance up the trail. Try to understand why the mammal has taken a specific route in reference to the overall terrain. Looking ahead on a fresh trail may allow you to detect the mammal before surprising it.

If you lose the trail, use your measurements of stride or group patterns to locate where the next set of prints should be. First, assume that the mammal continued in the direction it was traveling. However, if you don't see more tracks in that direction, check to make sure that the mammal didn't backtrack in its own prints. If that doesn't work, mark the last visible sign and start circling. Make little circles at first, but keep enlarging them until you pick up the signs again.

ELIMINATION

Finally, let me give you one last technique, the one I call elimination.

Sometime in your career, it will happen that you just can't make a positive identification of a mammal. The best thing to do at that point is to start down a mental list of mammal groups. As you do, determine how many of the clues fit each group. Then work within the most likely group and go through a mental list of mammals from that group one by one. When you finally chose one mammal, go over a mental list of what you know about it to see if it fits the picture.

CHAPTER ORDER

In the following descriptions of tracks, chapters and sections have been arranged in order by the number of toes registering in tracks; soft-padded mammals are first. The order proceeds from four toes, to mixed four and five toes, to five toes, to ungulates with two toes as follows:

Dogs	F4	h4	C
Cats	F4	h4	
Rabbits	f4	H4	cr
Rodents	f4	H5	
Bears	f5(4)	H5(4)	co
Weasels	f5(4)	H5(4)	co
Raccoon	f5	H5	co
Opossums	f5	H5	
Shrews	f5	H5	
Ungulates	f2	h2	

Notable variations in this general pattern occur, such as within the rodent order. Therefore always check the formula when referring to a family description.

This system allows you to quickly locate prints in the book by referring to the track formula at the bottom of each page. The system is also easy to learn as you try to organize your knowledge of tracking.

5. Dog Family

Members: *Domestic dogs, foxes, coyote, and wolf.*

Members of this family are digitigrade and, with their characteristic lope, cover many miles each day looking for food. Often they run their prey down. Track and trail patterns are relatively conservative, with many patterns differing only in dimensions among family members.

The front and hind feet may have a vestigial fifth toe on the inside, but only four toes show in the track. Claws are non-retractile and normally show in tracks (except in tracks of foxes, especially the gray fox).

Front feet are larger than hind feet. Four well-developed toe pads are separated from a large main pad that consists of one lobe in front and three in back. The overall shape of the track is longer than wide, providing the impression that the track is roughly rectangular.

The typical gaits of canids include a 2x trot and slow lopes. The 4x lope (gallop) is used; the "C-shaped" rota gallop is diagnostic for the dog family.

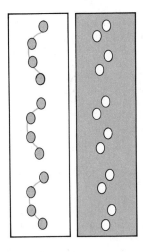

Gait patterns of canids:
A. A "C-shaped" rota gallop is most common.
B. A 2x trot with hind feet on one side of the line of travel.

Dog prints are rectangular in shape, have one lobe on the front of the pad, and usually show claws.

Fox

Foxes are more cautious than their larger canine relatives. They are adaptable and are found in most habitats, including the edges of large towns. Tracks show the foxes' hesitancy to cross large open areas. Foxes are the most playful canines, and their antics are often reflected in trails. The tendency to cache food is more evident in foxes than in coyotes or wolves.

Five species of foxes represent adaptations to a wide range of habitats: arctic tundra—arctic fox; deserts and grasslands—kit and swift foxes; forests and open country—red fox; and chaparral and rim country—gray fox. Kit and swift foxes are mostly active at night and will stay in burrows during the day. The red and gray foxes are often active during the day.

Foxes travel singly, in pairs, or in small family groups, but they do not form packs.

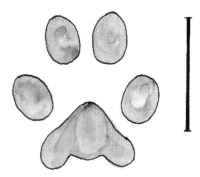

Occasionally claw marks do not show in prints of foxes (Canyonlands). Scale is 1 in (2.5 cm).

pletely cover the pads and fill in the spaces between the toes. The plantar pads on the hind foot of the red fox are almost completely covered with hair. More of the plantar pad shows on the front feet. During the winter, hair may completely cover the bottoms of the feet of the red fox.

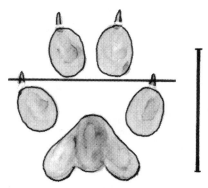

A delicate open print is characteristic of the gray fox (Moab, Utah). Notice the position of the toes in reference to the line. Scale is 1 in (2.5 cm).

Tracks are delicate, with a large space between toe pads and the main pad. Usually a line drawn across the anterior end of the outer toe pads will not intersect (or will only slightly intersect) the inside pads. Some or all the claws often do not register. This is particularly true for the gray fox, which has semi-retractile claws that allow it to climb trees.

The northern foxes (arctic and red) have relatively hairy feet that often make their tracks indistinct. The hair on the foot of the arctic fox may com-

The chevron-shaped pad and hair-covered foot are characteristic of the red fox (Red Desert, Wyoming).

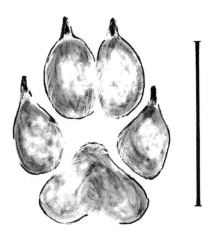

The print of the arctic fox, whose foot is also densely covered with hair, appears robust (Greenland). Scale is 2 in (5 cm).

The plantar pad of the red fox has a distinctive chevron-shaped (inverted "V") callous ridge showing through the hair. This pad, when visible, separates the red fox print from all other canids. Look in the bottom of the pad print for this ridge. On hard surfaces the chevron is the only portion of the heel that may show. Within a toe print, the smaller calloused toe pad may occasionally show. Compare the drawing of the red fox foot with its print.

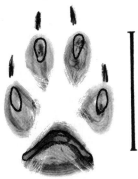

Careful study of the prints of a red fox will show the presence of callous pads in the bottoms of the pad impressions. (Canyonlands.) Scale is 1 in (2.5 cm).

Foxes often use the 2x trot, but the trail may appear strange at first. A fox holds its body at an oblique angle to the direction of travel. All front foot prints will be on one side of a line of direction, and the hind prints on the other side. A single fore foot print is obliquely paired with a single hind foot that is slightly forward in the line of direction.

Coyote

Coyotes adapt easily to different lifestyles and may be found in most habitats from high alpine to desert to inner city. Their daily wanderings cover many miles. Behaviorally, they are both bold and inquisitive. Look for coyote tracks crossing boldly and straight through open areas. The coyote investigates many nooks and crannies.

Coyotes use scent posts to communicate their presence in an area. Each prominent object will be scent marked with urine. Old carcasses are favorite locations even long after all nutritional material has been removed. Scats are also used for scent communications. When defecating, the coyote often scratches beside the scat, possibly to disperse its odor or an odor associated with glands on the feet. Scratching is done with the hind feet (see plate 6).

Generally, coyotes travel in pairs or as small family groups. When traveling as a pair, they often follow parallel routes up to 100 yd (91 m) apart. Packing behavior is not common.

Tracks are crisp, although extra hair is present in the winter. The relatively robust track is evidenced by the lack of space between toe pads and the main pad. The long axes of the toes remain parallel under most circumstances. Occasionally, there is a tendency for the inner claws to appear prominently in the tracks; often the outer claws do not register.

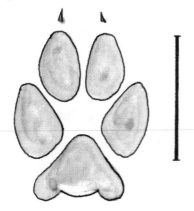

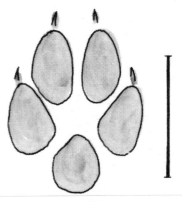

Often the smaller ends of the plantar pad do not show and it appears round. Scale is 2 in (5 cm).

Often the outside claws do not show in a coyote track. Scale is 2 in (5 cm).

The plantar pads on the hind feet are distinctly different from those on the front feet. The leading edges of the hind plantar pads tend to be **convex**, which reduces the size of the outside lobes. Many times, the outside lobes do not register, and a round impression is all that you will see in prints. The tendency toward a convex plantar pad on the hind foot is found in all canids but is most pronounced in the coyotes.

Wolf

Wolves have not demonstrated the ability to adapt to close association with humans as have other canids. They have now been restricted to the northern portions of the continent, and geographic location should be a primary clue to verification of wolf tracks. Wolves are bolder in their actions than other canids, and packing behavior is common. When traveling, especially in snow, **trailing** is common: the members of the pack follow in the exact trail of the leader to save energy. Scent posts are used to communicate territory boundaries. So is howling. Use your ears.

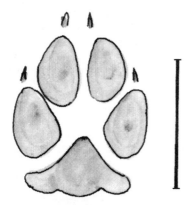

The leading edge of the plantar pad on the hind foot of the coyote is convex. This is true to a certain extent on other canids. Scale is 2 in (5 cm).

Tracks are very robust, especially in winter when extra hair fills the space between pads. Toes, especially on the fore feet, may tend to splay. Usually all four claws show in tracks.

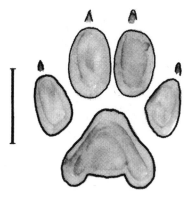

The front print of a wolf appears very robust (Denali). Scale is 2 in (5 cm).

DOG FAMILY COMPARISONS

Comparisons within the dog family are complicated by the genetic variation present in domestic dogs. Every pattern or trait observable in wild canids can also be found in dogs. There is no single trait or combination of traits that will absolutely distinguish dogs from wild canids. Rather, you must separate one from another based on the summation of clues, especially those showing behavioral adaptations.

Tracks of dogs reflect domestic living. Dogs have evolved with owners who provided supper when hunting was not successful. Therefore, dogs don't have to rely on stealth, and they tend to be sloppy walkers; hind feet seldom register directly on the front feet and may often be well to the side. Dogs approach strange or new objects directly without showing caution. Wild canids will circle the same objects, often to a downwind side, and approach cautiously. Toes often splay. Dogs have relatively larger tracks for their size than do wild canids. Extremely large tracks tend to belong to dogs rather than wolves because of this characteristic (for example, the tracks of a Saint Bernard).

Fox tracks and trails are relatively smaller in all proportions compared with those of other wild canids. Fox tracks are distinguished by their delicate nature. This dainty impression is due to the large spacing between pads (the hair-covered feet of the arctic fox being the exception). A line across the anterior edges of the outside toes tends not to intersect the front toes. This is not true for domestic dogs or other wild canids. A fox track as large as a coyote track will still lack robustness. Watch for playful activities in their trails.

Coyote tracks are relatively more robust than fox tracks. Less space exists between pads, and each pad is larger. The outer toes gives the impression of being larger.

Wolf tracks are very robust. Toe pads are much larger, and little space exists between pads. The inner toes appear bigger in tracks.

DOG FAMILY

F4 h4 C

Members	Front Foot				Walking			
	Length		Width		Stride		Straddle	
	in	(cm)	in	(cm)	in	(cm)	in	(cm)
Kit fox	1¾	(4.4)	1½	(3.8)	14	(36)	3 −	(7.5)
Gray fox	1⅞	(4.8)	1½	(3.8)	20	(51)	3¾	(9)
Red fox	2¼	(5.7)	2	(5.0)	25	(64)	4¼	(10.7)
Arctic fox	2¼	(5.7)	2⅛	(5.4)	30	(76)	4¼	(10.8)
Coyote	2½	(6.4)	2¼	(5.7)	30	(76)	5	(12.7)
Wolf	4¾	(12.1)	4	(10.2)	40	(102)	7 +	(17.7)

A plus or minus indicates that the track averages slightly larger (+) or smaller (−) than the measurement.

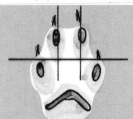

Red Fox Front Print.

- Claws generally show
- Prints longer than wide
- One lobe on front of pad
- Rotatory gallop is most common
- Compare robustness among members

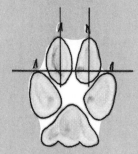

Coyote Front Print.

■ Outer toes bigger on coyote

Lines have been added to add in judging robustness and splaying.

Wolf Front Print.

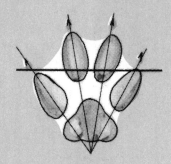

Dog Front Print.

6. Cat Family

Members: *domestic cats, bobcat, lynx, and mountain lion (cougar, painter, panther, puma, catamount)*.

Members of this family are digitigrade; their characteristic gait is a walk. Anatomically and physiologically, cats are not adapted for long periods of running, only short bursts of speed. Track and trail patterns are conservative, and size is a major differentiating clue between species.

A vestigial toe is found on the inside of the front foot, but only four toes show in each print. Claws are sharp and strongly curved for grasping and climbing. The claws are retractile and usually do not show in prints.

Front feet are larger than hind feet, and the plantar pads are relatively large. Toe pads are well developed and separated from a large main plantar pad. The plantar pad has two lobes anteriorly and three posteriorly. The anterior bilobing is diagnostic of the cat family. The overall shape of the print is round or wider than long.

When a cat is walking on hard ground, the hind foot registers in front of the fore foot. In snow, the tracks register exactly. For bursts of speed, cats gallop or jump. I have observed cougars using a rota gallop, but the most common pattern is a transverse gallop. When cats jump, one front print is often hidden under the hind prints, producing a 3x jump pattern. Rarely you may see a 2x trot pattern for short distances.

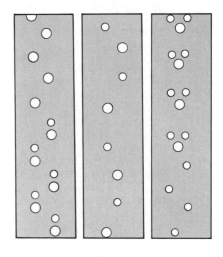

Common gaits for the cat family
A. Walk.
B. Rotatory gallop.
C. A walk changing into a 3x jump with one front print hidden.
Front feet are shown larger than hind feet.

Bobcat

Bobcats are very adaptable, and their behavior is similar to that of house cats. They are often found on the edges of towns. Their trails shows a preference for being near cover, and their playful nature is very evident. Bobcats will frolic with feathers and even blades of grass.

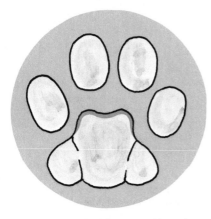

Cat family tracks show four toes without claws, appear round or at least wider than long, and have two lobes on the front of the plantar pad.

Bobcats are solitary and mostly nocturnal. Scent markings, urine, feces, and enhancement of excretion by scratching are used to maintain their social structure. There is a tendency for bobcats to cover their feces when on the hunting trail but to leave them exposed near their dens (see plate 7). Prey items may be cached by covering with available materials.

Bobcats are adapted to most habitats. However, they prefer rock piles and broken rock ledges, especially for denning. Home ranges tend to be small, less than 3.9 sq mi (10 sq km).

Tracks are crisp even in the winter. The print is delicate in appearance and appears very round. This effect may be enhanced by hair around the edges of the foot. Although the claws are retractile, I have seen claws in bobcat tracks going up hills and where the cats were jumping or making quick starts. The bilobed anterior edge of the plantar pad is usually apparent.

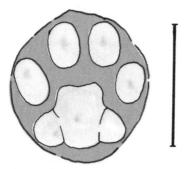

The impression left by the hair between and around the toes of the hind foot of a bobcat makes it appear rounder and fuller than normal. Tracks were in refrozen slush near Atlantic City, Wyoming. Scale is 2 in (5 cm).

F4 h4

Lynx

The lynx, often called Canada lynx, evolved in the northern regions. As an adaptation to the cold and snow, their cats' fur is thick, and their feet are densely covered by hair. Lynxes tend to avoid people, although I have found them visiting garbage dumps at a ski area and at a construction camp in Colorado. Their playful nature is also evident in their trails, and they will play with feathers and similar objects. Usually, lynxes are found not in the open but in dense cover.

Lynxes are solitary and mostly nocturnal, although in the winter they are about more during the day. Little is known about the marking behavior of lynxes. They will urinate often on the trail, usually on stumps or bushes. Scats are not covered. These markings may serve as territorial delineations. Ecological studies indicate that caching behavior is weakly developed; fewer than half of prey carcasses are cached, and those are poorly covered.

Lynx habitat consists of dense growths of conifers and associated rock outcrops. Deep snows and low temperatures are found in these areas, and in Colorado there is a slight preference for northern slopes.

Home ranges are small, though somewhat larger than those of bobcats. Lynxes, especially at times of population highs, have been known to travel hundreds of miles (kilometers).

Prints are seldom clear because of the dense fur that completely covers the foot. Much of the time, you can't distinguish the separate toes, and the plantar pad does not show. Drag marks made by the dense hair may be observed on either side of the prints. Lynx feet are unusually large for the animal's weight. These relatively large feet provide considerable advantage to the lynx when pursuing prey in deep snow.

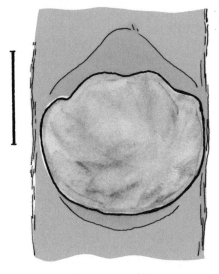

Lynx hind print in snow on the Frying Pan River, Colorado. The track is indistinct because of the densely haired foot. Hair drag marks are also visible on the outside of the track. Scale is 2 in (5 cm).

Mountain Lion

Mountain lions are known in different parts of the country by different names, including cougar, puma, painter, and panther (usually refers to the black

form). Their large home ranges usually require wild lands away from humans. Adequate supplies of deer are a prime requisite for populations to exist, and lions are one of the predators which eat porcupines. Grass, which makes up a large portion of their diet, is probably eaten for medicinal purposes.

Lions are mostly solitary and use **scrapes** to mark territories. Scrapes consist of local materials piled into a small heap with the hind feet. Urine and feces are often deposited on the scrape. Scrapes are usually located along travel ways. Prey items are often cached, and deer are dragged into ravines where they are covered with dirt, grass, and sticks (see plate 8).

Lion habitat is essentially that of their prey—deer. In the west, typical habitat is open woodland. Lions tend to prefer rocky cliffs and ledges and areas that provide cover—important for stalking their prey. Home ranges may cover hundreds of square miles (square kilometers).

The wide, deeply lobed plantar pad identifies the lion print. Scale is 2 in (5 cm).

The print of a lion is fairly clear and definitely robust. Overall shape is wider than long or round. Toe pads are relatively large, and prints of a fast-moving lion will occasionally show claw marks. Often the weight of the lion will obliterate the bilobing on the front of the plantar pad. However, the distinct and deeply three-lobed appearance of the trailing edge of the plantar pad is also an excellent clue. The plantar pad is relatively broader and more robust in respect to foot size than it is in canines. Under certain circumstances domestic dogs may leave prints that you could mistake for lion tracks—large dogs or hard ground. Check all the clues!

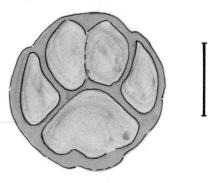

A lion print in the snow on South Pass, Wyoming. The great weight of the lion in the soft snow has obliterated the bilobing on the plantar pad. A hair imprint encircles the track. Scale is 2 in (5 cm).

CAT FAMILY COMPARISONS

The tracks of a large domestic cat may be hard to distinguish from those of a bobcat. Generally, bobcat tracks are larger and more robust. Location may serve as an additional clue, but feral cats are often found even in national parks.

The dainty bobcat tracks may be distinguished from lynx and lion tracks primarily by size. Both lynx and lion tracks are generally larger than 3½ in (9 cm), whereas bobcat tracks are seldom larger than 2¼ in (6 cm). Lynx and lion tracks are more robust and show wider and longer straddles and strides. An additional clue is the indistinct print of the hairy lynx foot.

Lynx tracks include the same size range as lion tracks, and both are more robust relative to the bobcat. However, the lynx is lighter in weight (15 to 55 lbs [7 to 25 kg]) than the lion (75 to 180 lbs [34 to 90 kg]). Since both mammals are supported on the same size foot, the lynx will not sink as deeply into the ground or snow. Their straddles may be similar, but the length of the stride is an excellent diagnostic clue. Lions have a long stride compared to the size of their foot print.

CAT FAMILY

F4 h4

Members	Front Foot				Walking			
	Length		Width		Stride		Straddle	
	in	(cm)	in	(cm)	in	(cm)	in	(cm)
Bobcat	2−	(5−)	2	(5)	22	(56)	5	(12.7)
Lynx	3¾	(10)	3¾+	(10)	28	(72)	7	(17.8)
Lion	3½	(9)	3½+	(9)	40	(102)	8	(20.3)

A plus or minus indicates that the track averages slightly larger (+) or smaller (−) than the measurement.

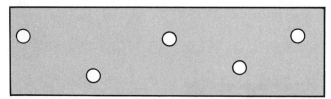

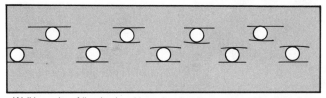

Walking gaits of lion (top) and lynx showing the greater stride of the lion.

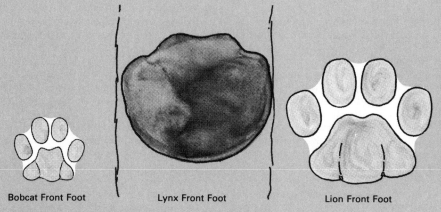

Bobcat Front Foot   Lynx Front Foot   Lion Front Foot

- Claws generally don't show
- Prints are round or wide
- Two lobes on front of pad
- Common gait is a walk

7. *Rabbit Order*

The lagomorph order consists of two distinct families: Ochotonidae, including the pikas, and Leporidae, including rabbits, jackrabbits, and hares. Lagomorphs are only distantly related to rodents, and they show many characteristics suggesting ancestry linked to the deer family. Order characteristics include soles of the feet mostly or completely covered with hair, digitigrade posture, tail small to not visible, and a second pair of incisors behind and reinforcing the front pair.

seldom registers in prints. Pikas commonly move by hopping. Because of the lack of soil in most rockfields, pika tracks are usually found in late-lying snow banks.

The densely haired feet of a pika from Niwot Ridge, Colorado, show toe pads on the tips. A fifth toe is present on the front foot (left).

Diminuitive hops characterize the pika. Scale is 1 in (2.5 cm).

PIKA FAMILY

Pikas, also known as rock rabbits and conies, have small ears, no visible tail, and hair covering all but the toe pads. A sharp "eee" sound in a rockfield near or above treeline is a prime clue to the presence of pikas. Pikas do not hibernate; instead, they store large haypiles for use during the winter. These piles are partially visible between rocks. Most of the time, pikas defecate at the same spot, covering the rock with a dense, white nitrogenous material. This white spot is, in turn, surrounded by bright, orange-colored nitrophilous **lichen**.

Tracks are indistinct because of hair on the feet. The hind foot is larger than the fore. Five digits are present on each foot. However, the first and smallest toe

RABBIT AND HARE FAMILY

Rabbits and hares are characterized by large ears, small tails, and hair completely covering the bottoms of the feet. Although pads are present, they are completely covered by strong springy hairs that point towards the toes. These hairs help cushion the foot when landing and provide greater surface area by spreading out.

Members of the rabbit subfamily give birth in a nest to **altricial** young, young that are born blind and naked. Jackrabbits and hares give birth to **precocial** young, young that are fully haired and have their eyes open at birth. Jackrabbits and hares do not construct nests but rest in **forms**, shallow depressions in the ground.

Tracks are indistinct because of hair on the bottoms of the feet. Although five toes are present on the front foot, the fifth toe rarely registers in prints. Much of the time, individual toes do not show in prints. The hind foot is longer than the fore foot. Leporids commonly use diagonal hop. Over long distances, their front feet occasionally change leads. When they walk, the heels of their hind feet may not register, leaving tracks that are similar in size and shape to the front prints. You may confuse these prints with those of dogs, cats, and weasels. The chevron-shaped plantar pad will help you separate leporid prints from those of dogs and cats. The symmetry of the plantar pads and evenly spaced toe pads differentiate leproid prints from those of weasels.

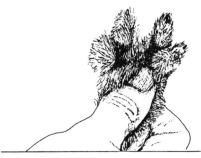

Pads are not present on the bottoms of feet in the rabbit family. Springy forward-facing hairs cover the foot of a cottontail rabbit from Sawhill Ponds, Colorado.

Trail of a snowshoe hare at the Mountain Research Station, Colorado, as it changes from a hop to a walk. Heel prints are not apparent when the hare walks on its toes. Scale ís 2 in (5 cm).

Rabbits

Rabbits survive by a strategy that includes both hiding and rapid, short-distance movements. They are seldom found far from their burrows or dense cover where they can disappear. Their reluctance to leave cover is reflected in their tracks, which seldom venture far into open spaces. Rabbits are very adaptable, and cottontails are often found living in towns, where their tracks on a snowy evening will reveal their unexpected presence.

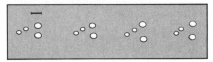

The diagonal hop of a rabbit showing small group and intergroup distances. Scale is 2 in (5 cm).

Rabbit prints are small and delicate. The hopping group pattern is also relatively short, even when the rabbit is moving fast.

Jackrabbits

Jackrabbits are animals of open areas, where they employ a strategy of fleeing at high speeds to escape danger. They are capable of traveling great distances, and their trails will be found crossing open fields. When pursued, they will travel in large circles a mile (1.6 km) or more in diameter. White-tailed jackrabbits turn white in winter, as do the hares.

The diagonal hop of a jackrabbit showing long group and intergroup distances. Scale is 2 in (5 cm).

Hares

Hares are found in northern or mountainous regions, where they turn white during the snow season (the exception being the Arctic hare which remains white year-around). Hares may be found from the densely-timbered areas of the mountains to the open flats of the tundra. Hares are mostly nocturnal, and we sense their presence by seeing their tracks.

The diagonal hop of the snowshoe hare. The hind feet are exceptionally wide. Scale is 2 in (5 cm).

RABBIT ORDER COMPARISON

The habitat of pikas will help differentiate their tracks from those of small rabbits. An occasional cottontail may be found in the home range of the pika. However, additional signs such as haypiles and scent posts will identify the territory of the pika.

The presence of rabbits is suggested by the relatively short intergroup distance of track patterns. This may be confirmed by the delicate nature and size of individual foot prints.

Jackrabbit tracks are more robust than the rabbit's, and the greatly elongated hind foot helps identify the jackrabbit. The hopping group pattern is also substantially bigger than that of the rabbits.

The prints of the hares appear more robust than those from other leporids, and the greater intergroup distance separates the hares from the rabbits.

In contrast to the other leporids, the snowshoe hare has an unusually wide and flexible hind foot. This wide foot, an adaptation to winter snows, serves as a snowshoe, preventing the snowshoe hare from sinking as it speeds over the light snow.

RABBIT ORDER

f4 H4 cr

| Members | Front | | | | Hind | | | | Hopping | |
| | Length | | Width | | Length | | Width | | Straddle | |
	in	(cm)	in	(cm)	in	(cm)	in	(cm)	in	(cm)
Cottontail	1 −	(2.5)	¾	(1.9)	3	(8)	1	(2.5)	11	(28)
Jackrabbit	1¾ −	(4.4)	1½ −	(3.8)	6	(15)	1½	(6.4)	20	(51)
Snowshoe hare	1¾ −	(4.4)	1½ −	(3.8)	5	(12.7)	3¾	(9.5)	19	(48)
Pika	¾	(1.9)	1 −	(2.5)	1	(2.5)	1 −	(2.5)	2	(5)

A minus (−) indicates that the track averages slightly smaller than the measurement.

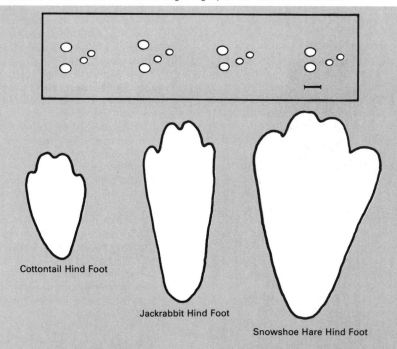

Cottontail Hind Foot

Jackrabbit Hind Foot

Snowshoe Hare Hind Foot

PIKA

- Large hopping hind feet
- Furry feet, toes indistinct
- Gait is a diagonal front foot hop

Note the five toes on the front foot

8. Rodent Order

If we measure success by the number of individuals or genera, then rodents must be considered the most successful mammals in the world. The rodents have diversified into a wide range of species including subterranean members that feed on insects and roots, terrestrial herbivorous and carnivorous forms, aquatic species with webbed feet, and arboreal members capable of gliding between trees. Nine families of rodents are present in North America, although the old world mice (Muridae) were introduced from Europe soon after North America was settled.

Rodents are only distantly related to the lagomorphs. Characteristics of the rodent order include a large open space between the incisors and molars **(diastema)**, and only one pair of incisors. The hind feet are larger than the front feet. The fifth toe tends to be reduced or lost from the front feet, and posture is plantigrade or semi-plantigrade. The larger members of the order retain the fifth toe on the front foot.

SQUIRREL FAMILY

Members: *tree squirrels, ground squirrels, rock squirrel, flying squirrels, chipmunks, prairie dogs, marmots, woodchuck.*

Considerable diversity is found within the squirrel family, and all but

aquatic niches are occupied by squirrels. Squirrels may hibernate in northern regions, estivate (deep torpor during hot periods) in southern regions, or be active year-round. Squirrels are herbivorous, but most will scavenge meat when possible. Ground squirrels, especially the golden-mantled squirrel, will actively prey on smaller animals when the opportunity exists.

When tracking squirrels, you should be familiar with those sciurids that hibernate in your area. Ground squirrel and chipmunk tracks are not common during the winter, although on a warm day, chipmunks may come out for a while.

The habits and relative size of the squirrels in an area will help in their identification. Tree squirrels form trails between their favorite trees, while ground squirrel tracks end in holes. Chipmunk tracks will seldom end at the base of a tree. The tracks of colonial squirrels cluster around their dens, but dispersing young and adventuresome males may often venture far from their burrows on a given day. Marked marmots on our study plots in Colorado have made round trips of over two miles in a single afternoon, including elevation gains of 2000 feet (600 m).

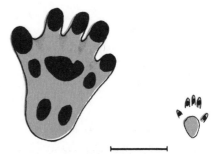

Relative size difference in the squirrel family is apparent in the hind feet of the chipmunk and the marmot. Scale is 1 in (2.5 cm).

Because squirrels are so small, tracks are often indistinct, but those found on suitable surfaces will be clear. The feet are not haired and all pads may show. Often, only the pads show and you must form a mental picture in your mind of the outline of the foot. This picture will simplify the task of understanding the story told by the tracks. The larger hind feet show all five toes, while the front feet show only four toes. There is a protusion on the front feet of larger squirrels that is a remnant of the fifth toe.

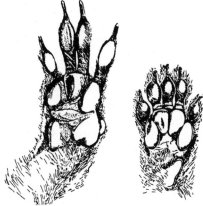

The front foot (right) of the gray squirrel shows four toes and a remnant pad instead of a fifth toe. Hind foot has five toes. Minnesota.

Squirrels move by bounding and use both the paired and diagonal hops. The main division that you will observe in tracking squirrels is the difference between those members that are arboreal and those that are terrestrial. The trails

of tree squirrels, which spend most of their life in trees, show paired front feet placed perpendicular to the line of travel. The prints of the front feet of ground-dwelling sciurids tend to alternate.

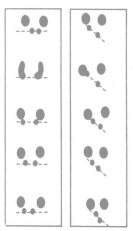

The paired front feet gait pattern (left) is characteristic of tree dwelling squirrels; the diagonal front feet gait is characteristic of ground dwellers.

In snow, squirrels tend to drag their feet and even their tails. Paired track patterns perpendicular to the line of

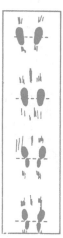

Various impressions that a squirrel may leave in the snow. Each set of tracks is a 2x pattern perpendicular to the line of travel. Drag marks are prominent going both into and out of the tracks. Often a tail drag is present.

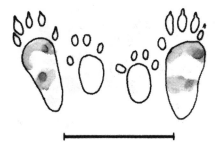

Typical 4x bounding pattern of the pine squirrel; front feet are paired. Pads on the hind feet show as slight impressions. Scale is 2 in (5 cm). Mountain Research Station, Colorado.

travel accompanied by drag marks are diagnostic. In shallow snow or soft dirt you can find frontprints separated from hind prints, but in deep snow the front and hind prints on each side merge to form two prints and occasionally all four prints merge into one. Again the drag marks will be your best clue.

BEAVER FAMILY

The aquatic habitat of the beaver provides an excellent source area for tracks. Complete tracks though, are hard to find because the hind feet usually register on the front feet and the tail drag will often obliterate both tracks.

Beaver feet are relatively hairless, and webbing is present between the toes on the large hind feet. I have seldom observed the fifth toe in a beaver's front foot print. Webbing marks are often present between the toes on the hind foot. Claw marks will often be present except on the second inside toe of the hind foot. The nail on this toe is modified so that it can be used as a comb to spread the **castor** (an oily substance produced by glands near the tail of the beaver) on the hair of the beaver. This process serves to oil the fur and make it waterproof.

When the beaver walks, its hind prints tend to obliterate the front prints. When both prints are visible, the front prints tend to be "pigeon-toed." The wide drag marks of the tail are often visible.

Beavers deposit their scat in the water where it disintegrates quickly. During the early morning hours, look carefully in and near the water for their scat. Backwater eddies are particularily good locations to find floating scat.

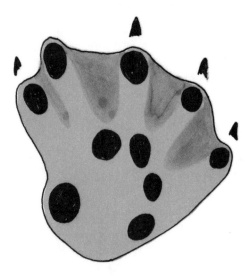

The hind foot of the beaver (left) shows webbing between the toes. A fifth toe may be evident in a clear front print. Teton Science School, Wyoming. Scale is 2 in (5 cm).

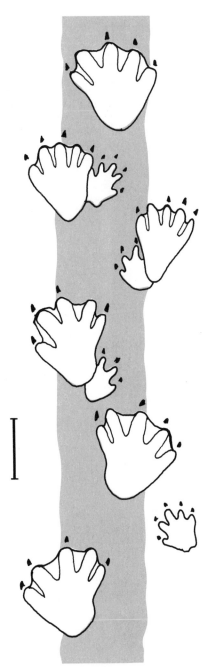

POCKET GOPHER FAMILY

Members: *pocket gophers.*

Pocket gophers (geomyids) and heteromyids (see kangaroo rat family below) are unique in the mammal world in that they possess external cheek pouches. The animals may place food into their fur-lined pouches without opening their mouths. Gophers may even chew without opening their lips because the incisors protrude through the skin outside of the lips. This allows gophers to chew on roots without getting dirt in their mouths.

Both families evolved in southwestern North America and have not dispersed far from their origins. The three genera of pocket gophers occupy subterranean niches from the desert lowlands to over 14,000 feet (4,200 m) in Colorado, where their distribution is restricted to soils suitable for burrowing.

Pocket gophers are usually detected by their summer mounds or winter castings. During the summer, the gophers push the soil that they have removed from their tunnels to the surface where it forms a conical **mound**. When the gopher finishes pushing the soil to the surface, it will close the tunnel behind itself. If you find tunnels into these mounds, you may be assured that the mounds are not occupied. Where you find occupied mounds, try to break into the tunnels. Then sit back and wait. You may gain a glimpse of this secretive creature when it appears to close the fresh break in its tunnel.

In the trail of a beaver, the front feet toe-in and may be hidden by the hind feet. Sometimes the tail may obliterate both prints. Teton Science School, Wyoming. Scale is 6 in (15 cm).

f4(5) H5 C

Castings (occasionally called **eskers**) are formed during the winter when snow covers the ground and the gopher does not have a place to dispose of soil from its burrowing activities (see Plate 12). I suspect castings are formed in the following manner. First, the gopher burrows out into the snow, forming a tunnel. If the snow from the tunnel is hard, it is carried below the surface of the ground to beneath the frost line where it melts. The gopher then pushes new excavated soil into the snow tunnel where it is packed into a hard casting. While excavating snow pits during the winter, I have found these soil castings several feet above the ground. When the snow melts in the spring, all the castings sink to the ground, giving the appearance that the original snow tunnels were at ground level.

Gophers also tunnel through the snowpack to reach nests and food caches. I have found caches of roots up to 20 inches (8 cm) in diameter when the snow melts in the spring. When the snow becomes waterlogged during the spring meltoff, gophers often die of hypothermia in their nests in the snow.

Gophers have naked, muscular feet with large, robust digging claws. The digging claws of the front feet extend well past the toes. Prints are seldom found because of the very loose nature of the freshly moved soil. I have ob-

served prints, though, in early fall snows when the young of the year were dispersing. In snow the trail of the gopher reflects the waddling gait of this stout little animal. A dragging imprint made by the thick tail may also be present between footprints. The snow on the sides of the trail appears pushed up, as if the gopher had burrowed through the snow rather than walked through it.

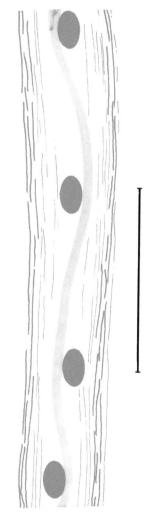

The trail of a pocket gopher in snow shows a tail drag mark. The edges of the trail are turned up as if the gopher burrowed through the snow. Scale is 2 in (5 cm).

The front foot (left) of the pocket gopher shows five toes. Niwot Ridge, Colorado. Scale is 1 in (2.5 cm).

KANGAROO RAT FAMILY

Members: *pocket mice, kangaroo rats.*

Pocket mice and kangaroo rats are adapted to the arid grasslands and desert regions of the west; they do not need drinking water, since they obtain all the water they need from their food. Like pocket gophers, members of this family are characterized by external cheek pouches. Heteromyids live in burrows and forage above ground at night. Seeds are carried back to underground caches. The presence of large auditory **bullae** (bones associated with the ears) indicates that their sense of hearing is well developed; this is perhaps an adaptation to night foraging in desert regions.

The presence of some kangaroo rat species may be indicated by earthen mounds up to 10 feet (3 m) in diameter. These mounds, which are used generation after generation, are formed when kangaroo rats scrape soil towards the center of the mound. Food caches and dens are located deep within the mound.

Look closely for slight depressions around the burrows of kangaroo rats. These areas are used for dust baths, which may serve to rid the kangaroo rats of fleas. Tracks register nicely in the fine dust of the bath.

Kangaroo rats have either four or five toes on the hind feet. The number of toes varies among the different species and may even vary within a single species.

Kangaroo rats often hop with their hind legs only and no front prints will be found. When the animal is moving fast, the hopping posture is digitigrade and the heel will not show in the print. When the animal is moving slower, the whole heel may show. This is especially true if the kangaroo rat is moving slowly enough for the front feet to be used. If the surface is soft, you may find an imprint of the tail, but when the rat is moving quickly the tail is often held high enough not to register.

In general, pocket mice are smaller than the other species of mice. Burrows are small and it is reported that there may be mounds of fine dirt near their entrances. Although I have live-trapped pocket mice in the Canyonlands country, I have never tracked these delightful little mice. If you have photographs or drawings of their tracks, I would be happy to receive copies.

R
O
D
E
N
T

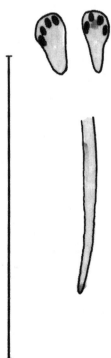

The hopping pattern of a kangaroo rat in Canyonlands. Only four toes show in the hind print but the long tail drag is evident. Scale is 6 in (15 cm).

f4 H5 (or 4)

JUMPING MOUSE FAMILY

Jumping mice are adapted to riparian habitats and are seldom found far from streams. When you approach one in the grass, it will leap away with large bounds and then freeze motionless nearby in the grass. If you approach carefully, you may be able to catch it in your cupped hands. No jumping mouse has ever tried to bite me (but there may be a first time). Jumping mice hibernate, so tracks will not be found during the winter.

Feet are hairless and relatively long, especially the hind feet. You must look closely in the mud on the edge of streams to find their tracks. You may see tail drag. The intergroup distance between hops is relatively great for a mouse of its size. Jumping mice tend to land on all four feet, not on two as the kangaroo rat does. Therefore, all four prints are usually found.

FIELD MOUSE FAMILY

Members: *deer mice (white-footed mice), harvest mice, grasshopper mice, woodrats (packrats), muskrat, lemmings, voles.*

Field mice native to North America form this family. Laboratory mice and rats and those that occupy human houses are, in general, old world mice (Muridae). This diverse family is composed of two subfamilies: the mice and rats (identified by their long tails, big ears, and big eyes) and the lemmings and voles (identified by their short tails, small eyes, and small ears). Bounding gaits are common, but lemmings and voles tend to walk more than other mice. Detailed studies of tracks and films of mice moving are needed before we will fully understand the dynamics of these small creatures.

The front foot (left) of the deer mouse shows only four toes. Sometimes only the pads register and not the whole outline. Scale is 1 in (2.5 cm).

Deer mice trails tend to show tail drag marks, but it is not always true as the deer mice also travel with their tails held vertically. The most common gait is a paired hop, indicating that deer mice are tree-climbing mammals. Although

The hopping pattern of a jumping mouse. Rocky Mountain National Park. Scale is 1 in (2.5 cm).

I have not verified it, I suspect that the trails of harvest mice also show paired front feet. Grasshopper mice place their feet diagonally. The short, stout tail of the grasshopper mouse probably does not leave a drag mark. Feet of all these mice are somewhat haired; excellent tracking conditions are necessary to find tracks that show detail.

Woodrats have only four toes (left) on the front feet. Canyonlands. Scale is 1 in (2.5 cm).

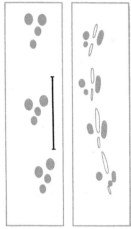

Deer mice when hopping may leave a tail drag (top) or they may hold their tails vertically, leaving none. Scale is 6 in (15 cm).

Woodrats are well adapted to the arid regions of the Southwest. The packrat of western stories is a bushytail woodrat. Nests up to six feet (2 m) in diameter in rock crevasses or buildings indicate their presence. Woodrats commonly bring in spines and pieces of cactus to their nest areas. In the desert, their nests are often built at the base of a cactus. These practices probably discourage other animals from digging into their nests. Another common woodrat sign is the presence of large masses of scat that have solidified into amorphous brown-black masses. White stains on the edges of rocks indicate repeated urination. Most people can smell the distinctive odor associated with woodrat dens. Use your nose.

The heels of woodrat feet are somewhat haired, and the tips of the toes are somewhat bulbous. Prints are roundish with extended heels. Woodrat trails show diagonal bounding.

Muskrats occupy aquatic habitats where they build underground nests. Occasionally they will co-habitate with beavers in the beaver lodge. Small dome-shaped mounds of grasses and sedges serve as warming huts and shelters. These domes may even be built on the ice cover of a lake.

There is a small rudimentary fifth toe on the front foot, which shows in very clear tracks. Muskrats waddle when they walk, and their tails leave an undulating drag mark between the prints. When the animal is bounding, it usually leaves a tail drag mark.

The trail of a muskrat showing a swagger and tail drag marks. Sawhill Ponds, Colorado. Scale is 5 in (12.7 cm).

Voles and lemmings commonly walk, although what has been interpreted as a walking pattern in these small mammals may in reality be a trot. Voles move with a diagonal hop. There is one exception to this—the red tree mouse *(Phenacomys longicaudus)* of the West Coast. This tree-dwelling vole leaves paired front prints. Lemmings also leave what appears to be a 1-2-1x loping pattern. Voles and lemmings seldom leave tail drag marks.

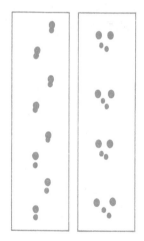

Common gaits of voles:
A. Walking gait where the hind foot oversteps the front foot.
B. Diagonal hop. The tail rarely shows in the trail of a vole.

Voles may produce castings similar to that of pocket gophers during the winter. Vole castings are smaller in diameter (less than an inch [2.5 cm]) and consists mostly of vegetation. Large caches of roots are not found in association with the vole castings. Voles tend to have well-defined latrines and scat will be found at one place. This is not true of gophers, which leave their scat in the castings, tunnels, and nests.

Voles and lemmings construct large nests of grass under the snow. When the snow melts off in the spring, you can count the nests and get an index of activity during the winter. The larger and best lined nests tend to be constructed by females with young. Weasels preying on voles and lemmings will take over the nests and line them with the fur of their victims. You should examine each nest closely and try to ascertain its history.

PORCUPINE FAMILY

Porcupines remove large amounts of bark and kill many trees in their efforts to feed on the cambium layer beneath the bark. "Porky" trees are identified by the presence of small pieces of bark and scat at the base. When the chewed areas are examined closely, small teeth marks will be apparent.

Clear prints of porcupine feet will show the rough texture of the bottom of the feet and marks from long hairs on the lower legs. Seldom do all the toes show. The trail is characterized by the short, waddling step and the tendency to toe-in. When you cannot see toe prints, you can identify the direction of travel by drawing lines through the long axes of the prints. The lines will form arrows pointing in the direction of travel. In deep snow, the porcupine will plow a furrow with its body.

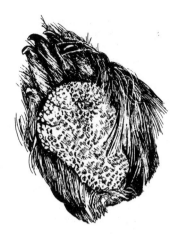

The surface of the foot of a porcupine is very rough. Pinedale, Wyoming. Sometimes you can even see the texture in a print.

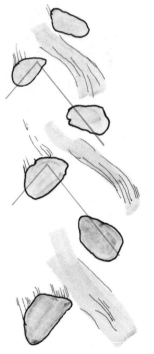

The pigeon-toed trail of a porcupine. Lines drawn through the long axis of the print form arrows showing the direction of travel. Tail drag marks are also evident. Long hairs may even register around each foot print. Yellowstone.

RODENT ORDER COMPARISONS

The great diversity found in the rodent order makes summary comparison difficult. Nearly every genus has characteristics that help distinguish it. Rather than review each of those characteristics here, I will show some of the traits and gait patterns that help to distinguish species or groups.

The rodent order is unified by the general shape of the foot which shows five toes on the hind foot and four on the front foot (see, however, sections on beaver, muskrats, and heteromyids). Relative size is a very important clue; for example, in the difference between a chipmunk and a squirrel.

In the hopping gaits, the position of the front feet is important. Those rodents that climb trees show trail patterns in which the front feet are paired and perpendicular to the line of travel. Those rodents that spend most of their time on the ground place their front feet at a line diagonal to the direction of travel.

The common gait of many rodents is a walk. (Perhaps if we knew more, we could separate some of the patterns we call walking into trots.) When examining walking patterns, you should look for drag marks made by a tail. Short-tailed rodents (voles) don't leave drag marks; long-tailed rodents (deer mice, woodrats, muskrats) do. The beaver leaves a broad tail mark. Porcupine trails often show drag marks left by the heavily quilled tail. Their foot prints may also show drag marks made by the heavy hair on the legs. Look for the toed-in walk of the porcupine and the beaver.

The champion hoppers, kangaroo rats and jumping mice, often show long tail drags in their tails. The long tail functions as a rudder during fast movements. Deer mice also show tail drags when hopping. Squirrels drag both the tail and the feet.

RODENT ORDER

Some rodents show a fifth toe on the front foot. Check the family to be sure.

f4 H5

The presence of claws in tracks varies from never to rarely to occasionally.

Members	Front Length in	(cm)	Front Width in	(cm)	Hind Length in	(cm)	Hind Width in	(cm)	Hopping Straddle in	(cm)
Squirrels										
*Tree	1	(2.5)	1	(2.5)	2	(5.1)	1	(2.5)	4¾	(12)
Chickaree	½	(1.3)	½	(1.3)	1	(2.5)	½	(1.3)	4	(10)
Flying	½	(1.3)	½	(1.3)	2	(5.1)	½	(1.3)	4	(10)
*Ground	⅝	(1.6)	½	(1.3)		(2.5)	¾	(1.9)	3½	(8.9)
*Chipmunk	½ −	(1)	½ −	(1)	⅝	(1.6)	½	(1.3)	1⅝	(4)
Beaver	3	(8)	2¾ +	(7)	5 +	(13)	5½	(14)	8	(20)
*Pocket gopher	⅝	(1.6)	⅝	(1.6)	1 +	(2.6)	⅝ −	(1.5)	1⅞	(4.8)
*Kangaroo rat	—	—	—	—	1 +	(2.6)	½	(1.2)	1 −	(2.3)
*Jumping mouse	⅜	(1)	¼	(0.6)	⅞	(2.2)	¼ +	(0.8)	—	—
*Deer Mouse	¼	(0.6)	¼	(0.6)	⅝	(1.6)	⅜	(1)	1	(2.5)
*Vole	⅛ +	(0.3)	⅛ +	(0.6)	¼ −	(0.6)	¼ −	(0.6)	1 +	(2.6)
Porcupine	2¾	(7)	1⅜	(3.5)	4 +	(11)	1½ +	(4)	8¾	(23)

*These measurements will vary depending on the species being studied.
A plus or minus indicates that the track averages slightly larger (+) or smaller (−) than the measurement.

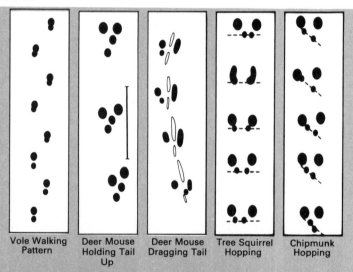

Vole Walking Pattern

Deer Mouse Holding Tail Up

Deer Mouse Dragging Tail

Tree Squirrel Hopping

Chipmunk Hopping

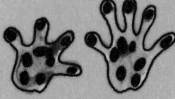

Front Foot

Hind Foot

Wood Rat

Tree dwellers place front feet opposite, while ground dwellers place front feet diagonally.

- Large hopping hind feet
- Front print 4 toes; hind 5 toes
- Hopping gaits are common

9. Bear Family

Members: *Black bear (cinnamon and brown), grizzly bears (including Alaskan and Kodiak Browns),* and *polar bear.*

Three species of bears are recognized in North America although considerable color and size variation may exist between subspecies. Even within one locality, you may see black, brown, cinnamon, and blond bears.

Bears are plantigrade and have non-retractile claws. Most of their time is spent walking and feeding. Track patterns are conservative and size is a major distinguishing characteristic among species. Other clues, including geographic locality, may be helpful. Bears leave other signs including **marking** or **rubbing trees** (see Plate 4).

Five toes are present on each foot. Their smallest toe, which is on the inside (not outside as in humans) of the foot, may not show in all tracks. The presence of claw marks in tracks is somewhat species dependent; claws often show in black bear tracks, usually show in grizzly tracks, and are rarer in polar bear tracks. Certainly the presence or absence of claw impressions in a print is not positive evidence of species. The hind foot is larger and distinctly different than the front foot. The metatarsal forms a distinct heel on the hind foot, giving a rectangular human-like shape to the print. The front foot is square in shape, and the intermediate pad is followed by a single metacarpal pad. The metacarpal pad is on the outside of the print, and the intermediate pad is also widest on the outside of the print.

The most characteristic gait is a walk. When bears walk, the hindfoot is placed in front of the forefoot. Remember that the little toe is on the inside of the print and does not always show. When moving fast, bears use either a transverse or rotatory lope. I have observed them

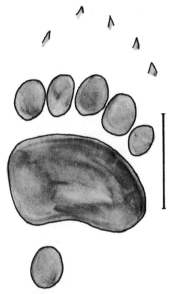

A clear print of the front foot of a bear shows the metatarsal pad. Scale is 4 in (10 cm).

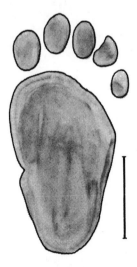

The hind foot of a bear with its long heel is very human-like. Scale is 2 in (10 cm).

f5(4) H5(4) co

using bounding gaits when going up steep hills.

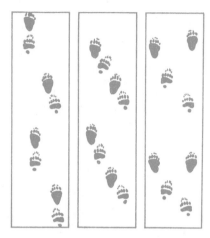

Common gaits of bears:
A. Walking gait where the hind foot oversteps the front.
B. Slow transverse gallop pattern.
C. Bounding pattern often seen on hills.

Black Bear

Black bears, when not hunted by humans, can live in close contact with civilization. Witness the situation in some national parks and the fact that black bears are active right up to the city limits of many towns in the west. The blacks are very adaptable and are omnivorous in their diet requirements. They are the least predacious of the bears, and plants form a large part of their diet. Animal matter you will see in their scat consists mainly of beetles and colonial insects—ants, termites,

and bees. Blacks climb trees readily. During the winter they go into a period of winter dormancy. Marking trees are common and marking activity tends to peak during the breeding season, indicating a relationship to the social structure of the bears (see Plate 4). Blacks are normally solitary except for adult females with cubs.

The toes of the front foot of a black bear form an arc over the intermediate pad. Scab Creek, Wyoming. Scale is 2 in (5 cm).

Black bear tracks vary from crisp to indistinct because some blacks have a lot of hair on their feet. Their toes are relatively loosely spaced and form a curved arc in front of the intermediate pad. Claw marks, when showing, will have a length about equal to or less than the length of the toe pads. The intermediate pad is wedge-shaped. In a clear front print, a single round metatarsal pad registers.

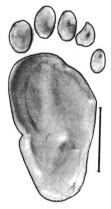

The hind foot of a black bear. Scab Creek, Wyoming. Scale is 2 in (5 cm).

Grizzly Bears

The constant pressure by humans and the need for relatively secluded spots have drastically reduced the grizzly's range in the twentieth century. Grizzly bears are now found in western Canada, Wyoming, Montana, Idaho, and Washington. A remnant population possibly still exists in Colorado. Locality should be the first clue considered when identifying possible grizzly tracks.

Behaviorally, grizzly bears can be very dangerous and aggressive, especially when with their young or when surprised. I recommend that anyone who is in bear country, especially grizzly country, read "Bear Attacks: Their Causes and Avoidance" by Steve Herrero (see bibliography). Herrero discusses bear sign in detail.

Grizzly bears may be found in a variety of habitats, but certain ones are preferred: alpine meadows, krummholtz, avalanche chutes, ridgetop glades, forest-meadow ecotones, and stream bottoms. The presence of scat is a prime clue! Grizzly (and black bear) beds are indicated by several scat piles in a small (20 yd [18 m] diameter) area (see Plate 11). The bed may just be a simple scrape or depression at the foot of the tree. Look for long kinky bear hair stuck to the tree bark.

The omnivorous grizzly eats plants, insects, fish, mammals, and human garbage (see section on scat). John Muir said of the grizzly that "almost everything is food except granite." The grizzly eats a large amount of plant material including grasses, forbs, berries, and nuts and is both a predator and scavenger on large mammals. Grizzlies also tear the bark of large trees to get at the cambium.

Grizzly bears will cache carcasses by partially covering them or even by lying on top of them. If you find a carcass, be aware that the grizzly is probably not far off, and you are in a very dangerous situation! The grizzly will defend that carcass! Grizzlies may remain on carcasses for two to three weeks.

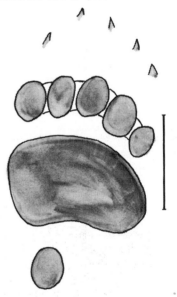

The front foot of a grizzly bear showing long claw marks. Yellowstone. Scale is 4 in (10 cm).

Grizzly bears are digging bears, and their claws tend to be long (3 inches (7.6 cm), especially the foreclaws. Grizzlies dig for roots, bulbs, corms, tubers, and small mammals. They tear rotten logs apart for insects. The grizzly also digs its own winter den rather than using a natural cavity. Grizzlies make extensive use of marking trees and will habitually use the same trails.

Grizzly tracks are crisp, although some hair grows between their toes. The toes are crowded together and form a relatively straight line in front of the intermediate pad. Toe pads are joined

f5(4) H5(4) co

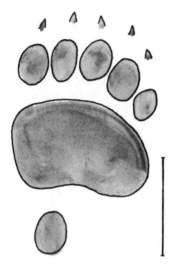

The claws on this grizzly were worn down and are very short in the print. Yellowstone. Scale is 4 in (10 cm).

towards the back of the foot. Because the toes are joined and crowded, the sides of toes may appear to be straight and parallel to each other. In a very clear print, the joined toes may be visible.

The claws, especially on the front feet, are very long. They tend to be twice as long as the toe pads and will usually show in the prints. However, remember when the bear is doing a lot of digging (in the spring for roots or in the fall for a den), the claws may be worn down to short stubs and may not even show.

The walking trail of the grizzly is very wide, and in areas where they use trails habitually, you may see separate worn spots where the bears step. When moving quickly, grizzlies will leave a loping pattern.

f5(4) H5(4) co

Polar Bear

Polar bears, the largest and most predacious of the bears, are found around the rim of the polar basin. Known denning areas are present in Alaska, Hudson Bay, Baffin and Ellesmere islands, and Greenland. Polar bears seldom stray far inland away from the pack ice. They may even live for years on the pack ice without coming to shore.

Females den in snow drifts during the winter to give birth to young. Dens are of two types: complex dens where females give birth, and temporary dens used after the mother and her young have abandoned the **maternity den**. Non-pregnant females and other bears seldom den. Polar bears do not go into a period of torpor during the winter. Most of their diet consists of seals, but some small mammals, birds, bird eggs, and plants are taken when seals are not available. Polar bears will scavenge on carcasses of larger mammals, including whales. Polar bears may behave aggressively towards humans.

Polar bear print from Baffin Island, Canada. Photo by Jay Stravers. Scale is 8 in (20 cm).

In Greenland, I have photographed the bottoms of a polar bear's feet as it was rolling in the grass to dry off. The foot was massive and toes were closely packed. Even during the summer, extensive amounts of hair were present, but the pads were bare. However, due to the rocky soil, I could not obtain tracks. Track drawings presented here are from a slide taken by Jay Stravers on Baffin Island. Tracks may be indistinct due to the dense hair on the feet.

Toes form more of an arc over the intermediate pads than you will see in grizzly tracks. Claws tend not to show in tracks.

BEAR FAMILY
COMPARISONS

Identification of bear tracks can be difficult because of the conservative nature of their track patterns. Whenever possible, look for clues other than tracks to help clarify identification. See the section on scat for further differentiating clues. Since it is often impossible to positively separate black bear and grizzly bear sign (especially if you are a new tracker), it may be best to assume that all bear sign in grizzly country was made by a grizzly bear, and act accordingly—*cautiously*. A wrong identification and a surprise encounter with a grizzly may cost you your life.

There are no size criteria that will positively separate the sign of a black bear from that of a grizzly! Don't believe anyone who says there are! The sign of an adult female grizzly may easily be mistaken for an adult male black bear. And if that female grizzly is with her cubs or surprised, that mistake may be fatal. Be careful when working in grizzly country. Again, read Herrero.

Tracks of black bears are generally smaller than those of grizzlies. As a guideline, tracks smaller than five inches (12 cm) wide may be adult black bears (but see grizzlies below). The claws on the front feet offer the best clues for species identification. Claws on the front feet of the black bear, when present, are short—usually less than about 1.25 inches (3 cm). Often, claw marks do not show in black bear prints. However, the absence of claws or the presence of short claws does *not* positively identify a black bear print. I have photographic slides of black bear prints

with long claws and many photographs of grizzly bear prints *without* claws.

The tracks of grizzly bears are more robust and larger than black bear tracks. Tracks wider than 5 inches (12 cm) are probably grizzly. However, Herrero presents data on female grizzlies with foot widths starting as narrow as 4.3 inches (10.9 cm). These females were all accompanied by cubs. Claws, when present on the front foot, are generally longer than 1.4 inches (3.5 cm). Claw marks in grizzly tracks, if they have not been shortened by digging form a pointed chevron with the longest mark above the center toe. This chevron is also somewhat apparent in the hind foot print.

The best clues for separating black and grizzly prints, though, are the greater arc of the toes in the black bear and the joining of the toes in the grizzly. In the front print of a black bear, a line drawn from the base of the big toe (outside toe) across the top of the intermediate pad will intersect the little toe at the mid-line or above. The same line drawn on a grizzly bear track will tend to intersect the little toe below the midline or not at all. Look closely to see if toes are joined at the base. Joined toes when visible in tracks identifies the grizzly.

Grizzlies are the digging bears. Extensive digging in an area identifies a grizzly. By the same token, the presence of roots, tubers, etc. in scat indicates a grizzly and not a black bear.

The toe prints in polar bear tracks tend to form a greater arc over the intermediate pad than do those of the grizzlies. Polar bear tracks are generally larger than grizzly tracks, and claws may show less frequently. Of course polar bear tracks are found close to the ocean on the rim of the polar basin. Any tracks out on ice floes are probably polar bears.

B
E
A
R

BEAR FAMILY

f5(4) H5(4) co

Members	Front				Hind				Walking	
	Length		Width		Length		Width		Straddle	
	in	(cm)	in	(cm)	in	(cm)	in	(cm)	in	(cm)
Black bear	4½	(11)	4	(10)	7	(18)	3½	(8.9)	14	(36)
Grizzly	5½	(14)	5	(13)	10	(25)	6	(15)	20	(51)
Polar bear	5¾	(15)	9	(23)	12	(31)	9	(23)	??	??

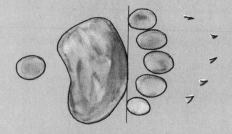

Two gait patterns
- Walking patterns
- Slow lope pattern

In a grizzly print, a line drawn from the big toe across the top of the intermediate pad intersects the little toe below the middle or may not intersect at all (after Palmisciano).

Black Bear

In a black bear print, a line drawn from the big toe across the top of the intermediate pad intersects the little toe at or above the middle (after Palmisciano).

- Hind print is human like
- Little toe may not show
- Claws don't always show
- Metacarpal pad on front foot
- Common gait is a walk

COLOR PLATES

The color plates illustrate animal behavior that the tracker may identify when tracking mammals. You will better be able to interpret mammal trails when you can visualize their behaviors, because the animal actions often provide other signs and additional clues in the tracks. Try to "see" the animal in its trail and visualize the position of its body. When you can "see" the animal, the story told by its trail will be clearer.

1. Wolf scent marking. Canids, territorial animals, mark their territories by scent marking. The leg-lift posture is often assumed. However, only the dominant alpha male and female wolves use the leg-lift when scent marking; subdominant wolves of both sexes squat to urinate. All male coyotes use a leg-lift when urinating. The position of the urine stain in reference to the position of the hind legs may help identify sexes (see page 31).

2. Beaver cutting trees near its pond. The workings of the beaver are familiar to most of us. Chewings of other rodents can be confused when they are located near the beaver's aquatic home. Large tooth marks up to ¼ inch wide (0.6 cm) identify trees and branches that have been chewed by the beaver. Look closely at each set of tooth marks so that you can identify the fine division between the front two incisors. Tooth marks from porcupines, while they may be of similar size, are usually found higher in trees. Chewings by other rodents can be identified by small tooth marks. Beavers chew trees at an angle to the trunk, not parallel to it. Porcupines sitting in trees may chew parallel to the trunk.

3. Elk scraping antlers on a tree. Each fall, members of the deer family rub trees to remove the velvet from their newly grown antlers. Saplings, the usual victims, are often bent double and occasionally snapped. Bark is stripped off and small branches are broken. The ragged edges of the remaining bark will separate rubs from chewings by rodents; rodent chews show sharply cut bark.

When cervids debark trees to get at the sap, they do it by raking their lower incisors up the trunk. They do not chew the bark off the trees. The lower edge of the bark will be sharply cut and the upper edge more ragged because cervids don't have upper incisors to bite off the bark strip.

4. Grizzly bear clawing an aspen. Bears mark trees in three manners: they will scratch their backs on the trunks, they will remove large patches of bark to get at the sap, and they will claw the trunks. When large areas of bark have been removed, look for claw marks at the upper edge of the patch. We do not know why bears claw trees, but I believe that there is probably some communication function involved. Claw marks on trees, especially aspen, will last many years. Remember, as trees grow, they continually increase in diameter. Claw marks made by black bears will, with time, reach the proportions of those made by grizzlies and even larger.

5. Snowshoe hare browsing on a conifer branch. The large hind feet of the Colorado snowshoe hare remain white even in the summer. Snowshoe hares often feed on conifer twigs, and twig remains may be found associated with their scat. Hares are capable of biting off large twigs with a single bite. Smaller rodents take several bites. Winter chewings may be high on the sides of trees as the hare will be working from a platform of snow.

6. Coyote scratching near its feces. Feces may be used as an additional method of territorial marking by coyotes. Once they have defecated, coyotes often scratch near their scat. The scratching may serve to dissipate fresh odors, and the exposed scat may serve as a long-term territorial marking. Scratching is done with the hind feet.

7. Bobcat covering its feces. When hunting and far from the den, bobcats tend to cover their feces. They do this by raking dirt over the feces with their front feet. Nearer their dens, bobcats tend not to cover their feces. Exposed scat may serve as a territorial marking.

Mountain lions tend to behave similarily, but lynxes tend not to cover their scat.

8. Mountain lion caching a deer. A mountain lion will drag its kill into a ravine, under a tree, or under a ledge where it covers the carcass with dirt, grass, and sticks. While standing on or behind the carcass, the lion uses its front feet to rake material over the kill. Even if there is not much material present on the surface, the lion may still attempt to cover the kill. The lion will remain near the carcass for a few days as it finishes its meal. Often the cat will stay on the carcass when approached closely by humans.

9. Otters "playing" on lake surface. When traveling, otters often slide on their stomachs. They are capable of sliding, not only down hills, but even on level areas such as frozen lakes. The otter places all four feet on the ground and dives forward. As it slides, the front legs are held parallel to its sides. Slips may be 20 feet (6.1 m) or more in length. Also note the 2x bounding pattern with the tail drag marks.

10. Black-footed ferret making a trough. Ferrets will excavate large amounts of dirt in their attempts to find prairie dogs. During excavation, they make distinctive troughs by moving the dirt away fom the burrow. Troughs are positive proof of ferrets in a prairie dog town, and most troughs are made from December through March.

11. Black bear leaving its day bed. During the day, bears "bed" for short periods. Their beds, while in the forests, are often near clearings. The bed may be nothing more than a shallow depression scraped in the ground or in a rotting log. Examine depressions for the bear's long, fine, kinky hairs. If the bed has been used by an ungulate, the hairs will be long, coarse, and undulating. Only a few hairs may be present in either case. Get down on your hands and knees and look closely. Beds may be used for several days, especially if food is nearby. Bears deposit scat in close proximity to their beds and often many piles may be present.

12. Pocket gopher moving dirt from its burrow. The pocket gopher shoves dirt from its burrow with its front feet. When all of the freshly dug dirt is out of the burrow, the gopher will close the opening it is working through. Gophers never allow the opening to remain open for more than a few minutes. Portions of the castings from the previous winter are visible in the upper portion of the picture. Of particular interest are the large incisors which close outside the lips! This arrangement allows the gopher to chew on roots without getting dirt in its mouth.

10. Weasel Family

Members: *weasels, marten, fisher, wolverine, mink, otter, ferret, badger, and skunks.*

The weasel family, mustelids, shows an almost unbelievable range of adaptations, including ground dwelling weasels (three species of weasels and the wolverine), arboreal hunters (marten and fisher), aquatic **piscivores** or fish eaters (mink and otter), burrowing or **fossorial** members (black footed-ferret and badger), and malodorous **omnivores** that eat many insects (three species of skunk). Habitat will help you identify species.

Behaviorally, members of the weasel family are inquisitive and ferocious. Mustelids are relatively fast and strong for their size. They will often attack and kill animals larger than themselves. All members possess anal scent glands. The skunks spray the liquid scent. Mustelids tend to be active predators but will scavenge. The wolverine is more adept at scavenging than predation.

All three weasel species turn white in the northern portions of their ranges during the winter. When white, they are commonly called ermine.

Corresponding with the wide range of life styles, there is a wide range of tracks and trails. Members range from digitigrade to plantigrade and share some common characteristics.

In general, mustelid tracks appear slightly wider than long. Hind prints of the plantigrade mustelids appear human-like with long and prominent heels. You get a slight impression that their toes are crowded.

Mustelids have five toes on both fore and hind feet. Much, but not all of the time, the five toes will show in a print. Occasionally, the smallest toe, number 1 or the inside toe, will not register. The toes tend to display a 1-3-1 spacing, with toes 1 and 5 separated slightly from the other three toes. The spacing is diagnostic and is apparent in many prints. With practice, you can identify the 1-3-1 spacing in most prints, including the more plantigrade members of the family (i.e. skunks), where toes are closer together. The spacing will help you separate mustelid prints that show only four toes from those of coyotes and bobcats. A single metapodial pad is present on the fore foot of digitigrade mustelids, although it does not always register.

The 1-3-1 spacing of toes is characteristic of mustelid prints. Even though one toe does not show in the mink print on the left, the 1-3 spacing is apparent. Scale is 1 in (2.5 cm).

Mustelids have well-developed claws that often show in prints. In some prints, only a few or even none of the claws will show. Digging mustelids, badger and skunks, have well-developed front claws that register well in advance of the toes.

Hind foot of a striped skunk, Colorado.

f5(4) H5(4) co

Semi-retractive claws may only partially show (mink track on left) or may be readily apparent in the digging members (striped skunk, Great Sand Dunes, Colorado). Scale is 2 in (5 cm).

The fused interdigital pad is chevron-shaped (inverted "V") in all but the skunks (less so in otter). The fore foot has a single metacarpal pad which often does not register in prints.

Metacarpal pad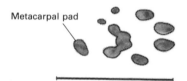

The fused interdigital (plantar) pad of the mink shows distinct asymmetry in size and shape. A metacarpal pad is present in clear prints. Scale is 1 in (2.5 cm).

In skunks, the chevron tends to be more filled in, and two metacarpals are present. The pads on the hind foot form a nearly continuous sole. The pads of skunk feet are better developed and may give the impression of one fused interdigital and one fused metapodial pad.

Hair on the bottom of the feet may be dense during the winter. This is especially true of martens.

A marten print in winter showing the effect of dense hair. Scale is 2 in (5 cm).

Two gaits are typical of the weasel family. The smaller mustelids and those animals moving fast tend to show a 2x bounding pattern. This pattern is the result of the "humping" movement observed in pet ferrets and results from the hind feet being placed directly on top of the front prints once the fore feet have been moved. The 2x bounding pattern is at an angle to the line of travel, which helps differentiate the pattern from that of the squirrels. Large mustelids and those mustelids moving slowly show a 1-2-1x lope (gallop).

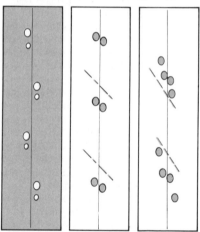

Common gaits of the weasel family
A. Skunk walking.
B. 2x jump used when moving fast or by smaller mustelids.
C. 1-2-1x lope used when moving slowly or by larger mustelids.

Skunks and badgers tend to walk more than other mustelids. Otters (and occasionally minks) move by sliding on their stomachs on snow-covered slopes or ice-covered lakes.

Weasels

The three species of North American weasels, listed from largest to smallest, are the long-tailed, short-tailed, and the least weasel. During the winter, white-colored weasels are called ermine, but to the scientist only the short-tailed weasel is an ermine. Weasels are perhaps the most curious members of the mustelid family. Their trails seldom go far in a straight line and show continual changes in direction corresponding to slight changes in stimuli. Weasels investigate everything in their range and stick their heads into every little hole. The slender body of the weasel allows it to pursue mice and voles deep into their own holes or runways. You may find their trails crossing large open areas and/or in dense vegetation.

Sexual dimorphism exists between the sexes with the males being distinctly larger. Size differences between species are not clear cut, and the males of the smaller species overlap in size with the females of the larger species. For instance, track measurements taken during the winter in Jackson Hole, Wyoming, show a slightly tri-modal distribution of sizes for the long-tailed and short-tailed weasels, with long-tailed males and short-tailed females at the extremes. The female long-tails overlap with the male short-tails. Therefore, it is not always possible to separate species by print size. In areas where only one species is present, it may be possible to reasonably identify sexes by size of prints.

Individual prints are delicate. However during the winter, extra hair on the feet will make them appear more robust and indistinct. Most tracks found during the winter will not show individual toes and are best identified by the characteristic 2x bounding gait.

In snow, weasels tend to drag on every other jump. This leaves a dumbell-shaped pattern with a space before the next pattern. Weasels also tend to burrow in the snow, and many trails

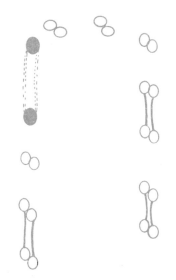

The wanderings of the weasel are revealed in its trail which burrows below the snow and makes right angle turns. The dumbbell pattern is characteristic of the weasels.

will disappear below the snow only to reappear again a short distance away. It is not unusual for a weasel trail to make an abrupt right angle turn. When not in the snow, weasels may leave a jumping pattern reminiscent in shape of rabbit prints.

Marten and Fisher

Martens and fishers are closely related mustelids which are adept at moving in the trees. Both pursue and take squirrels for food. Martens also eat other small mammals, birds, insects, and fruits. Predominant foods for the

W
E
A
S
E
L

f5(4) H5(4) co

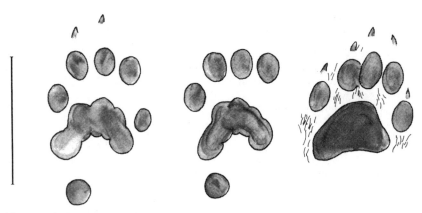

Marten tracks may show either four or five toes in prints. During the winter, dense hair makes the prints appear more robust. Prints are from the Mountain Research Station, Colorado. Scale 2 in (5 cm).

fisher are porcupine, snowshoe hare, rodents, and carrion. While martens are chiefly nocturnal, fishers are active day and night. If you are tracking and lose the trail of either animal, make large circles because both mustelids will travel from tree to tree, not leaving footprints on the ground. Fishers are, in general, simply a larger, darker version of the marten.

The tracks and trails of fishers are similar to those of martens but somewhat larger. You will see considerable variation in size, but the description for the marten will suffice for both species. Prints of both species are most robust than those of the weasels. Tracks seldom are clear during the winter because of dense hair covering the feet. The hair tends to wear off towards spring, making pads more visible. Since individual prints tend not to show toes in the winter, size and the 2x bounding pattern are the best clues.

f5(4) H5(4) co

Wolverine

Wolverines are the largest terrestrial members of the weasel family. They are not common anywhere, and their range has been considerably reduced since the turn of the century, although populations exist in Minnesota and in the central Rocky Mountains as far south as Wyoming and possibly in Colorado. Wolverines are adept scavengers and travel great distances each day looking for carrion. Their keen noses can detect carrion under several feet of snow. Powerful jaw muscles allow them to crush bones as large as the thigh of a moose, and the size of broken bones is an important clue. They are active mostly at night.

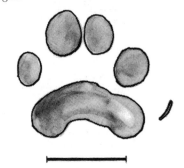

Even the largest land mustelid, the wolverine, may only register four toes. Look closely for the fifth toe. Aspen, Colorado. Scale is 2 in (5 cm).

Tracks are very robust and wide. The metapodial pad on the front foot usually registers in a good print. You can confuse the width of the wolverine track and trail with only four other mammals: the wolf, lynx, lion, and possibly bear. Typically the wolverine uses a 1-2-1x lope (gallop), although 2x and alternate fore foot jumps are observed. Even though the wolverine is a large mammal, averaging about 25 to 30 lbs (10 to 14 kg), the inside and smallest toe often does not register.

The front foot of a wolverine showing mustelid characteristics: 1-3-1 spacing and asymmetrical plantar pad, Utah. Scale is 2 in (5 cm).

Otter

Otters are found almost exclusively near lakes and streams. Occasionally they travel for extended distances over land, but this may simply represent travels of the dispersing young. Otters mainly feed on fish, crayfish, insects, and amphibians. Otters are sociable, and family units often travel together.

Tracks are usually observed on the water's edge or on frozen lakes during the winter. Prints are relatively crisp year-round. This is, I believe, because the relatively warm water during the winter does not necessitate additional hair on the feet.

The regular gaits of the otter include the 2x bound and 1-2-1x lope (gallop). Otters will also slide on the snow and mud banks. Slides, known as **slips**, are fairly distinctive and occur not only on hillsides but also on the flat ice of frozen lakes (see plate 9).

The full length of the hind foot often registers, leaving a definite heel impression in prints. However, sometimes otters walk in a digitigrade manner and the heel does not show. A sure clue is the webbing on the hind foot. Look closely between the toe pads for signs of the webbing.

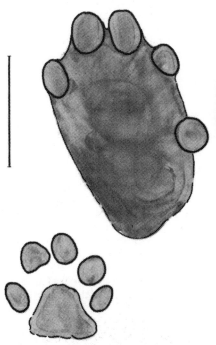

The heel print often shows in the plantigrade otter print, but if the animal is moving fast on its toes, the heel may not show. Webbing may appear between toes. Tracks from Yellowstone and South Carolina. Scale is 3 in (7.5 cm).

W
E
A
S
E
L

f5(4) H5(4) co

Mink

Minks, aquatic mustelids, are closely related to the weasels but are significantly larger. Minks are seldom found far from water, where their principal diet items include fish, muskrats, birds, crayfish, mice, and amphibians. Activity is chiefly nocturnal. Minks generally travel alone.

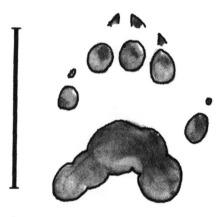

Print of a mink in Yellowstone. Scale is 1 in (2.5 cm).

Tracks are most often found in the mud or snow at the water's edge. Prints are less distinct in the winter. The most common gait used by the mink is a 2x bound and secondly the 1-2-1x lope. Minks will slide down banks as do otter, but the slip is much narrower. Minks also dive under the snow to emerge short distances away. They may travel under the river ice during the winter, surviving by using air pockets.

`f5(4) H5(4) co`

Black-footed Ferret

Few people have the opportunity to see ferrets in the wild, let alone the opportunity to track them. I am indebted to Tim Clark, Denise Casey, and Louise (Richardson) Forest for most of the information presented here. The black-footed ferret is the rarest mammal in North America and, as I write this, its status is currently in doubt. As of December 1985, three known animals remained in the wild, and there were about six that had been captured for breeding attempts. During the summer and fall of 1985, distemper decimated the only known population, near Meeteetse, Wyoming. Recent estimates had been over 100 animals in the prairie dog towns.

Tracks of black-footed ferrets resemble those of minks. In good tracks all five toes will show. The typical gait is the 2x bound; in some cases a tight 1-2-1x lope is observed.

Other signs left by ferrets include digging and troughs in excavated dirt (see Plate 10). Digging rates are highest from December through March, the period of hibernation in white-tailed prairie dogs. The number of digs per night averages about 0.6. Ferrets tend to go to the tops of prairie dog mounds to urinate. Movements during the course of a night's activity average about 1500 yd (1400 m). Under proper snow conditions it may be possible to identify the tracks of large males. Scat is only occasionally found, typically at or near burrow openings. Tail marks may result when ferrets stand on their hind feet to observe the surroundings.

Badger

Badgers are active predators, digging out fossorial ground squirrels and pocket gophers. As opportunistic feeders they also eat other small mammals, such as mice and voles (a major item in some areas), insects, birds, and reptiles. Badgers often hunt in partnership with coyotes. The coyote will stand near the surface entrances to catch any fleeing prey. If the luckless creature turns back into its burrow, the badger is waiting. Badgers eat carrion and cache food in old dens. At dens that are used for longer periods, the badger temporarily closes the entrance with soft dirt, known as **throwing a plug**. They can also throw a plug when pursued into a burrow. However, less than half the active badger burrows will have a plug. Dens where young are raised have unusually large amounts of soil in front of them.

The body of the badger is adapted to digging, and this is reflected in its prints and trail. Badgers are low to the ground and have a wide body with larger digging muscles in the shoulders. They normally walk with a plantigrade swagger with the toes turned-in. However, badgers can move surprisingly fast and have been observed moving through tall sage, occasionally jumping above the brush for a clear view. While hunting, they may travel five to eight miles during a night, leaving a trail of freshly dug holes.

Clear prints are hard to obtain because of their swaggering gait. The hind foot usually registers, at least in part, on the fore print, and the pattern of the two prints appears long and merged. Individual toe pads also appear elongate. The fore feet have very long (2 in or more [5 cm]) and strong claws for digging. The claws register in the tracks well in front of the toes.

The long digging claws of the badger are apparent in its pigeon-toed trail, Jackson Hole, Wyoming. Scale is 2 in (5 cm).

f5(4) H5(4) co

Skunks

The skunk group includes a variety of mammals that spray a bad-smelling liquid from glands located near their anuses. Five species of skunks comprising three genera are found in the U.S. and Canada. The genera are spotted skunks (*Spilogale*), hog-nosed skunks (*Conepatus*), and striped and hooded skunks (*Methitis*). A variety of common names have been applied to the skunks including polecat and civet. The spotted skunk has also been called hydrophobia cat, weasel skunk, tree skunk, four-stripe skunk, and black marten. The spotted skunks are smaller and more agile than the other two genera, and can climb trees.

Skunks are omnivores. Their diets include insects, carrion, rodents, small rabbits, frogs, crayfish, lizards, fruit, and other plant materials. Hog-nosed skunks will root for insects and grubs, earning their nickname, rooter skunk. Spotted skunks feed more on rodents and small rabbits than do the larger skunks. The larger skunks are not fast enough to pursue prey; they hunt by lying in wait or stalking prey.

Skunks do not cache food but will raid the caches of other mammals especially the weasels. The extensive diggings of the hog-nosed skunk give away its presence. Other skunks leave only small pits when they dig. Piles of scat will often indicate the presence of skunks.

Skunks may dig their own burrows but seem to prefer to use burrows already constructed by other animals.

They will nest in houses, walls, basements, culverts, and other structures. In the colder regions, they go into a torpor (dormancy) during cold snaps.

Skunks are plantigrade and seldom hurry. Animals with such a potent defense as the skunks, don't have to hurry! Their behavior reflects a slow and meandering lifestyle, with walking patterns that are often erratic. The length of many steps may be shorter than a normal walking gait. When traveling long distances, the larger skunks commonly use a 1-2-1x lope, while the spotted skunk has a greater tendency to bound.

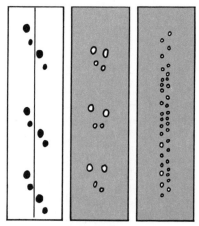

Common gaits of skunks
A. 1-2-1x lope by a striped skunk.
B. Bound by a spotted skunk.
C. Short spaced walk (crawl).
     Hind feet are larger.

Skunk tracks are often indistinct due to sloppy walking and the presence of long hairs on the feet. The long claws on their front feet are well developed for digging and may help you identify their front prints when the metacarpal pads don't show. Claw lengths are 3/4 inch (20 mm) or more for hog-nosed skunks, 2/5 inch (10 mm) for striped skunks, and 1/4 inch (7 mm) for spotted skunks.

The muscular feet, which evolved for digging, leave prints with little space between pads. The metatarsal pads on

The front print of a striped skunk from Great Sand Dunes shows long digging claws. Scale is 2 in (5 cm).

the hind feet of the spotted skunk are separate, but in the other skunks they are joined.

Olaus Murie found that the toes of the hog-nosed skunk were longer than those of other skunks. He also reported that the walking gait of the spotted skunk produced a "puttering" track pattern with very short steps.

WEASEL FAMILY COMPARISONS

Small mustelids and mustelids moving fast will tend to leave a 2x bound print. Larger mustelids or those that are moving slowly will tend to show a 1-2-1x lope pattern. The plantigrade and slow-moving mustelids will have a greater tendency to show the heel in their prints. For instance, when they are moving slowly otters will show the heel in the hind foot patterns, but as speed increases they move more up on their toes and the heels will not show. Therefore, when making comparisons, try to estimate the speed of the mustelid because the size of the tracks may depend on speed.

The size of prints will help to separate the three species of weasels. In some areas, it may be possible to distinguish the large males from the smaller females. All weasels tend to leave a drag mark between pairs of tracks. This "dumbbell-shaped" pattern is not observed in the other mustelids. Otters will leave slide marks, but these are much longer than the length of the normal stride.

The hind foot of a striped skunk from Colorado shows the extensive development of the foot pads. Scale is 2 in (5 cm).

WEASEL FAMILY
f5(4) H5(4) co

Members	Front Length in	(cm)	Front Width in	(cm)	Hind Length in	(cm)	Hind Width in	(cm)	Bounding Straddle in	(cm)
Weasels										
Least	⅜	(1)	½ −	(1.3)	⅜	(1)	½ −	(1.3)	1½	(3.8)
Short-tailed	½	(1.3)	½ +	(1.3)	½	(1.3)	½	(1.3)	2	(5)
Long-tailed	¾	(1.9)	¾ +	(1.9)	¾	(1.9)	¾ +	(1.9)	2½	(6.4)
Marten	1¾	(4.4)	1¾ +	(4.4)	1¾	(4.4)	1¾ +	(4.4)	3½	(23)
Fisher	2½	(6.4)	2½ +	(6.4)	2½	(6.4)	2½ +	(6.4)	6	(15)
Wolverine	4	(10)	4 +	(10)	4	(10)	4 +	(10)	9	(23)
Ferret	1⅛	(2.9)	1¼	(3.2)	1⅛	(2.9)	1¼	(3.2)	2½	(6.4)
Badger	2½	(6.4)	2 +	(5.1)	2	(5.1)	2	(5.1)	10	(25)
Mink	1¾	(4.4)	1¾ +	(4.4)	1¾	(4.4)	1¾ +	(4.4)	2¾	(7)
Otter	3¾	(9.5)	3¾ +	(9.5)	3¾	(9.5)	3¾ +	(9.5)	9	(23)
Spotted skunk	¾	(2)	1	(2.5)	1¼	(3.2)	1 −	(2.3)	2¾	(7)
Striped skunk	1½	(3.8)	1¼	(3.2)	1⅞	(4.8)	1¼	(3.2)	3½	(9)

A plus or minus indicates that the track averages slightly larger (+) or smaller (−) than the measurement.

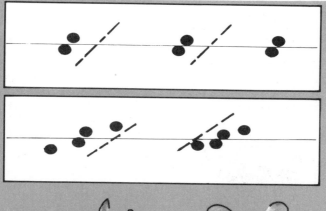

Plantigrade Foot of Skunk

Long Digging Claws of Skunk

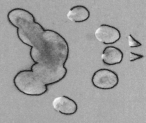

Wolverine Front Print

- 1-3-1 spacing between toes
- Little toe often doesn't show
- Plantar pad is asymmetrical
- Common gaits are 2x jump and 1-2-1x gallop at an angle
- Claws may not show

11. Raccoon Family

Members: *coati, raccoon, and ringtail.*

The raccoon family is a diverse and loosely-related group of mammals of the western hemisphere. Three species occur north of Mexico: *coati, raccoon,* and *ringtail.* All three species are omnivorous, but ringtails consume more animal protein than the other species.

Foot posture varies from semi-plantigrade (ringtail) to plantigrade (raccoon and coati). Gaits and track patterns are variable. All species have five toes on the fore and hind feet, and all toes show in the tracks. Hind tracks are larger than front tracks. The bottoms of raccoon and coati feet are hairless. Some hair is present on the bottom of ringtail feet. Claws are well developed and non-retractile except for those of the ringtail which are semi-retractile The overall shape of the foot varies and is characteristic of the species.

Raccoon

The raccoon is a very successful generalist which is found throughout the U.S. and into southern Canada. However, its range does not extend high into the mountainous portions of the west. Raccoons will be found in many cities, where they live in the storm drains. Raccoons are omnivorous and opportunistic in their feeding habits.

They consume many species of plants and animals and in many areas plants are more important in the diet than animals are. Raccoons are very adept at catching aquatic organisms that they feel under water with their sensitive toes. Raccoons go into a period of torpor usually associated with the first permanent snow cover each winter. During warm spells lasting several days in the late winter, they may come out to forage. Raccoons are nocturnal but may return to their dens an hour or two after sunrise when feeding. Piles of scat may function as home range markers but we know little about this.

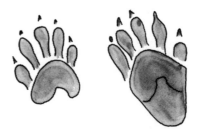

The tips of raccoon toes are bulbous. The hind print (right) looks like a human footprint and the front print is somewhat hand-like. Hobcaw, South Carolina. Scale is 4 in (10 cm).

Tracks are crisp and characterized by widely-spaced toes, which are bulbous on the tips. The toes on the fore feet are somewhat elongate and with the bulbous tips appear very finger-like. The prints may look like miniature hand or footprints and are longer than they are wide. Claws usually show at least in front of some toes. The heel pad (metatarsal) of the hind foot often does not show well in prints. The typical gait of the raccoon is a rolling walk in which the hind print registers close to, usually beside, the alternate front print. This is not a pace form of the trot but a rolling walk. When tracking raccoons, remember that they are excellent tree climbers.

The walking pattern of the raccoon shows the front foot opposite the hind foot. Boulder, Colorado.

Coati

The range of the coati (also called coatimundi) extends from Central America into the southern U.S. Animals up to two years in age roam in bands of as many as 20 individuals. Older males accompany these bands only for a short time during the mating period. Bands break up about June. Coati are mainly diurnal.

Although I have had coatis destroy my live traps while working in Saguaro National Monument, I was not able to track them because of the rocky soil. My notes on coati tracks come from

plaster casts in the Murie collection at Teton Science School. The tracks of a coati compared to a raccoon of similar size are not as large because the toes of the coati are not elongate. The coati does not have the bulbous toes that the raccoon has. Coati tracks appear longer than wide. Coatis can climb trees.

The print of the coati is robust with five toes and claws showing. Murie collection. Scale is 2 in (5 cm).

Ringtail

The ringtail differs from raccoons and coatis in many respects. Some of these have already been mentioned. Pairs of ringtails may be observed at all seasons, and both parents tend to the young after they are about three weeks of age. Ringtails live in a wide variety of rocky and woody habitats. In Colorado, they have been observed up to the high montane zone, but they prefer drier areas. They are active mainly at night.

The track of the ringtail is very cat-like, being round in outline. However, you will see five toes in clear prints. Tracks are relatively crisp, although hair may obscure some prints. The toes of ringtails are tightly packed, and the semi-retractile claws may or may not

Common gait patterns of the ringtail:
A. A 4x bound with the hind feet on the outside.
B. A rotatory gallop.

Ringtail tracks are round and cat-like. Five toes show and the metatarsal pad identifies the front foot (top). Canyonlands. Scale is 1 in (2.5 cm).

show, depending on how they are being held. The metatarsal heel pad helps distinguish the hind print from the front. In Canyonlands, I have observed tracks indicating slow bounding movements. However, these agile mammals are capable of faster gaits. Ringtails climb trees and are very adept on rock faces.

RACCOON FAMILY COMPARISONS

The tracks of raccoons, coatis, and ringtails are quite distinctive and easy to tell apart. Raccoon tracks, generally the largest, are distinguished by elongate toes on the front print and bulbous tips on all toes. Coati tracks are large and longer than wide, whereas the tracks of the ringtail are small, dainty, and round.

R
A
C
C
O
O
N

RACCOON FAMILY
f5 H5 co

Members	Front Length in	(cm)	Front Width in	(cm)	Hind Length in	(cm)	Hind Width in	(cm)	Walking Straddle in	(cm)
Ringtail	1+	(2.5)	1+	(2.5)	1+	(2.5)	1+	(2.5)	3	(7.5)
Raccoon	2½	(6.4)	2½	(6.4)	4	(10)	2¼+	(6)	10	(25)
Coati	1½	(3.8)	1¼	(3.2)	1¾	(4.4)	1⅝	(4.1)	??	??

A plus (+) indicates that the track averages slightly larger than the measurement.

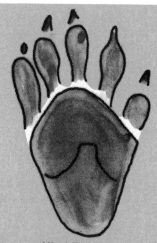

- Five toes on all feet
- Claws may show

Raccoon Hind Foot
- Bulbous tips on toes
- Hand and foot like

Raccoon Front Foot

Ringtail Front Feet
- Compact roundish tracks
- Claws generally don't show

Coati
- Robust track
- Several animals in a group

12. Opossum Family

Opossums are the only marsupials in North America. Females have an abdominal pouch where they nurse their young until they are large enough to care for themselves. Opossums are om-

nivorous and will eat anything they can find.

The tracks of the opossum are distinctive. The toes of the front foot spread widely. The hind foot resembles a miniature hand in having an opposable inside toe that is separate from the outside toes. The opposable toe lacks a claw; because claws seldom show, however, this characteristic is not too helpful. In prints, the opposable toe is directed to the side or even to the back. Often the walking gait resembles that of a raccoon in that the front foot appears opposite the diagonal hind foot. The front foot, however, may also register in front of the hind when the opossum is walking.

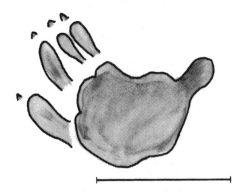
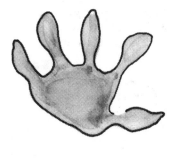

The print of the opossum appears hand-like. The "thumb" on the hind print (left) is separated from the other toes and does not have a claw. Scale is 2 in (5 cm).

13. Shrew Family

Shrews are active little insectivores that do not hibernate during the winter. They occupy a wide range of habitats from riparian zones (river and stream areas) to arid grasslands and deserts. Several genera are found in western North America, ranging in size from the tiny dwarf shrew to the large water shrew. Water shrews are the size of smaller mice.

The tracks of shrews differ from those of rodents in having five toes on the front feet. Since it is usually hard to distinguish the number of toes, size may be the principal criterion for separating shrew prints from those of mice. Gait patterns are similar to, but usually smaller than, those left by mice. When hopping, shrews appear to show paired front feet, indicating that they are at home climbing trees. The appearance of pairing, however, may be because of the small size and difficulty in distinguishing paired imprints from diagonal ones. More information is needed about this. Tail drags are often present in walking and hopping gait patterns.

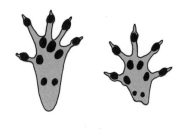

Five toes are present on both feet of the shrew. Often only the pads will show in a track; in a clear print, however, the overall outline may register. Scale is 1 in (2.5 cm).

The hopping gait of the shrew is very mouse-like, but the intergroup distance is very short. Three hops fit into a 6 in (15 cm) distance.

14. Even-Toed Ungulates

Members of this order represent a diverse group of herbivores. Four families compose the order: peccary, antelope, sheep, and deer. The foot has evolved for speed, and foot posture is unguligrade with four digits on each foot (however, see peccary and antelope). Feet are cloven and front feet are larger than hind feet.

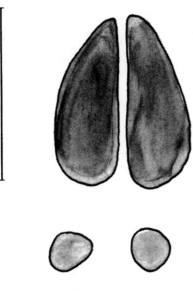

The cloven hoof is characteristic of ungulates. Dew claws may show in prints. Scale is 4 in (10 cm) on this elk print from Colorado.

PECCARY FAMILY

Members: *peccary (javelina)*.

Peccaries are pig-like mammals of the Southwest. Mainly vegetarian, they will occasionally feed on snakes and are apparently immune to rattlesnake bites. Peccaries are gregarious and live in small bands. They usually feed during the cooler hours of the day or at night. During the hot part of the day, they will seek shelter in a thicket, under a boulder, or in a limestone cave. They also seek shelter and give birth in burrows dug by other animals or in hollow logs. Peccaries frequent waterholes.

One dew claw is found on each hind foot. Prints are small and delicate. The overall outline is rounded as are the tips of the hoof. However, dew claws do not show in the prints. The usual gait of the peccary is a walk.

Peccary print from plaster cast in the Murie collection. Scale is 1 in (2.5 cm).

DEER FAMILY

Members: *deer, elk, moose, caribou (reindeer)*.

Male members of the deer family and female caribou have **antlers**. These bony structures are shed each year and are regrown in time for the fall rutting season.

Four digits are present on each foot, but the dew claws often do not register in the tracks. They will register for larger animals or when the animal is on softer ground. The presence of dew claws in a track does not indicate a male animal. Dew claws are farther from the hooves on the hind feet than on the front feet. Front feet are larger than hind feet, and when the animal is moving fast or on soft ground, the front feet splay more than the hind feet.

Common gaits include walking and rota gallops. When walking, the animals tend to drag the front of their hooves as they move forward.

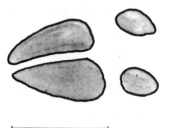

Dew claws may show even in a mule deer print (Lake Powell, Utah). The surface was soft mud. Scale is 2 in (5 cm).

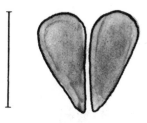

Overall a deer print appears heart shaped. Lake Powell. Scale is 2 in (5 cm).

Deer

Two species of deer are recognized in North America: the mule deer and the white-tailed deer. Mule deer are found in the open areas of the western half of North America and are identified by their large ears and symmetrically forking antlers. White-tailed deer are found over most of the forested, lower portions of North America except in the dry Southwest. Their antlers branch from one main beam. When moving away from you, white-tails display their prominent white flag high above their rump.

The "average" print of a deer tends to be "heart-shaped" and the outline tapers to a sharp point. There is great variability, however. You should also learn to recognize the broadly splayed and therefore non-heart-shaped print of

deer. Larger bucks tend to have larger prints than does. In many areas where hunting pressure is heavy, though, the older, larger bucks may be absent. Where both "white-tails" and "muleys" occur together it is not possible to tell prints apart. Habitat preference may help as white-tails prefer forested and riparian areas, while mule deer prefer mountains and more open spaces.

In addition, the gaits of the deer may help to distinguish them. Mule deer have a tendency to **stot** more than white-tails. Since all four feet move simultaneously during the stot, the hind prints register behind the front prints. White-tailed deer tend to use a galloping gait in which the hind prints register in front of the front prints. Remember, both species can use any of the gaits mentioned and it is the summation of all clues that provides the final indentification. Although I have not been able to check it, I sense that white-tailed deer may show a greater tendency to use a transverse gallop than do mule deer.

F2(4) h2(4)

H 𝟎𝟎 𝟎𝟎 H	𝟎𝟎 F	𝟎𝟎 F
F 𝟎𝟎 𝟎𝟎 F	𝟎𝟎 H	H 𝟎𝟎
H 𝟎𝟎 𝟎𝟎 H	H 𝟎𝟎	𝟎𝟎 H
F 𝟎𝟎 𝟎𝟎 F	F 𝟎𝟎	F 𝟎𝟎
H 𝟎𝟎 𝟎𝟎 H	𝟎𝟎 F	𝟎𝟎 F

Common gaits of deer:
A. Stot with little horizontal movement.
B. Rotatory gallop.
C. Transverse gallop.

Other signs may be helpful in determining the sex of a deer that you are trailing. During the rut, bucks are likely to urinate on the front legs and scent glands. As a result urine may drip on the snow between foot prints. Where deer have been browsing, look for imprints from the antlers, as the tips may drag in the snow when the deer gets a mouthful of food. Also look for rubbing trees and branches that the bucks have attacked with their antlers. Although, I have heard that does with their more graceful walk will not leave drag marks in less than 3/4 inch (2 cm) of snow, I have not been able to verify this.

Elk (Wapiti)

Elk are found mainly in western North America but have now been introduced into many areas in the east and south. Elk tracks are robust. The outline of the print and the tips of each half of the hoof are broad and rounded. Dew claws often show and the prints of bulls tend to be larger than those of cows. I have observed more transverse galloping patterns than rota gallops.

During the rutting seasons, rubbing trees and wallows will be found. Wallows are formed by the elk "**horning**" the ground, pawing the ground and rolling in the resulting depression. Wallows used over several years may develop into small lakes in areas where the water table is high. Bull elk also urinate on the scent glands of their fore legs during the rut. Again urine spots on the trail may indicate a bull.

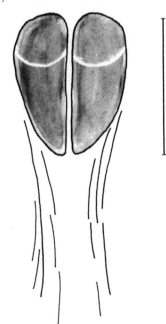

Elk print showing drag marks from the front of the track. Slightly rounded depressions from the pad may register at the rear of the print. Notice how thick and robust the tips are. Mountain Research Station, Colorado. Scale is 4 in (10 cm).

D E E R

F2(4) h2(4)

Elk debark trees by raking their lower incisors up or across the trunk. These scrapes can be separated from rubbing trees by the presence of teeth marks. The remaining bark on rubbing trees is ragged in appearance. Aspen seem to be a favorite item in the elk's diet. Aspen that are gnawed repeatedly will soon develop a black scarred bark indicative of heavy use.

Moose

Moose are found in the northern regions of North America and southward down to the central Rocky Mountains. Their tracks are remarkably delicate for such a large mammal. The width is narrow and the hoof tips are pointed as is the general outline. Large dew claws help to spread the weight of the moose out over a greater surface area when it is walking in the soft mud of its riparian habitat. Because of the moose's great weight, dew claws often show in the prints of both sexes. Therefore, the presence of dew claws in prints does not indicate a bull moose.

I have observed moose trotting and galloping when they must move fast. The trot is common for short distances, while the gallop is less common and may be reserved for emergencies. I once observed a moose being run on Jackson Lake by snowmobilers. The galloping pattern that it left was remarkedly long and indicated the great speeds that a moose is capable of.

Moose will **highline** trees in the winter as they do not move far each day. Their favorite winter food is willow. Since members of the deer family do not have upper incisors, you may identify willows that have been browsed on by their crunched tips. Limbs eaten by rodents or snowshoe hares will show distinct bite marks. Larger diameter branches may be broken when the moose pulls them down to get at the tender tips. Moose also use rubbing trees in the fall to get the **velvet** (hair and skin) covering off their antlers.

Caribou (Reindeer)

Caribou evolved in the northern region where large hooves were beneficial on both winter snows and summer muskeg. The large circular hooves prevent caribou from sinking into the surface. The circular shape and spreading nature is diagnostic.

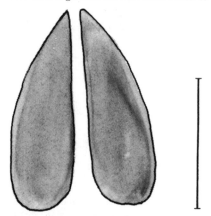

The print of the moose, though large, is delicate and pointed. Yellowstone. Scale is 4 in (10 cm).

F2(4) h2(4)

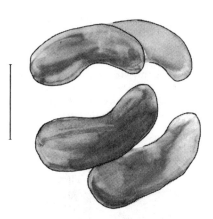

Caribou prints are round in overall shape and round at the tips. The hind print registers over the front one in this print from the Murie collection. Scale is 2 in (5 cm).

SHEEP FAMILY

Members: *mountain sheep, mountain goat, muskox, bison.*

Members of this family have true **horns** consisting of bony cores covered by a sheath of hardened material derived from hair. They are non-branching and neither the core nor the sheath is shed. Both males and females have horns. Dew claws are present but they often do not show.

Mountain Sheep

Two species of wild sheep are found in North America: the bighorn and the Dall sheep. I have never had the opportunity to track Dall sheep, so the information presented here is for bighorn.

The prints of bighorn are blocky with rounded tips. Edges tend to be straight and the overall outline appears wedge-shaped. The sole of sheep hooves is softer and more concave that that of other artiodactyls. This is reflected as a raised, half-moon-shaped area in the center of some prints.

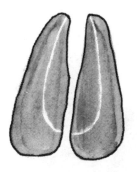

Sheep prints have straight sides and blunt tips. Overall they are wedge-shaped. Concavity is apparent in this print. Scale is 2 in (5 cm). Gros Ventre Canyon, Wyoming.

Mountain Goat

Mountain goats, whose original distribution was northwestern North America, have been introduced into many areas to the south. Their original southern limit was northern Washington, Idaho, and Montana. The tracks of mountain goats tend to be relatively short compared to their width. The outline is blocky, the square shape caused in part by spreading of the tips. Tips are pointed, but this may be hard to see in the tracks.

D E E R

F2(4) h2(4)

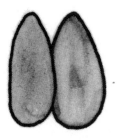

Goat prints are blocky and relatively wide. Tips are pointed. Mt. Evans, Colorado. Scale is 2 in (5 cm).

is rounded but flattened lengthwise. The prints are very robust and cannot be confused with other tracks on their native range. The tracks are similar to those of domestic cows. During the two summers I worked in Greenland, I only observed muskox walking and cannot report on the track patterns of their faster gaits.

Bison (Buffalo)

Bison have made a remarkable comeback from the remnant herds that survived at the turn of the century. They may now be found in many parks and preserves throughout North America. The tracks are very robust and the tips of hooves are pointed. The overall out-

Muskox

The native range of muskox is restricted to north central Canada and Greenland. However, muskox have been reintroduced into many parts of Alaska and Canada. The tips of the hooves are blunt on the ends and the fronts are scarcely more pointed than the hind portions. The overall outline

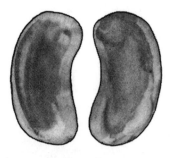

The print of the muskox is round but flattened lengthwise. Ella Island, Greenland. Scale is 4 in (10 cm).

The overall shape of a buffalo print is round but each half of the hoof is narrow (compare with the width of the muskox). Scale is 6 in (15 cm). Yellowstone.

line is rounded. The wall is very hard and the sole soft. Often on hard surfaces, only the outline of the wall will show

F2 h2

and the front separation between the halves of the hoof will not be obvious. In these cases buffalo tracks may be confused with horse tracks. When moving fast, buffalo use a transverse gallop almost exclusively.

Buffalo wallows are common and have a dramatic effect on the landscape. Landscape patterns created by buffalo wallows have survived for over 100 years on the Konza tall grass prairie in Kansas. Wallows are used throughout the year and not just during the fall as they are with the cervids. Rubbed and horned trees also occur.

Antelope Family

The pronghorn antelope family is **endemic** to (found only in) North America. It is the only North American species with forked horns. The outer sheath is shed annually. Horns may be present in both sexes. The number of digits has been reduced to two on each foot, and no dew claws are present.

The pad of the antelope is well formed and round. The rear of the print is wide and the tip narrow. This is evident in the outline of prints if you look closely and develop an average picture of the trail you are following. Study the drawings carefully because it takes a discriminating eye to detect the rounded pad characteristic. Overall, the outline of the print is blocky.

I have only observed antelope using a rota gallop and believe that the rota gallop may be more exclusive to an-

telope than to members of the deer family.

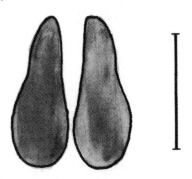

The rear of the antelope print is rounded and the tips are narrow. Walden, Colorado. Scale is 2 in (5 cm).

Artiodactyl Order Comparisons

Where ranges of similar artiodactyls overlap, a set of prints can be hard, if not impossible, to positively identify (for example, mountain sheep, goats, and antelope). You will have to pay close attention to details and try to form an "averaged" picture of the trail that you are following. Consider the habitat first; then evaluate relative size and shape. Tracks are compared by similar groups and increasing average size.

Peccary tracks are delicate and rounded. Dew claws may show but only one per hind foot. Antelope prints will show the large rounded pad at the rear of each half of the hoof and a narrow tip. Toes tend not to splay. Antelope do not have dew claws.

Mule and white-tailed deer have prints that are heart-shaped in outline. Tips are pointed and dew claws show in soft ground. Elk prints are robust and rounded. The pad is small, taking up only the rear portion of the track. Once you know where to look for the pad in an elk print, its position will help separate elk prints from those of moose. Dew claws may show in elk prints. Moose prints are long but delicate. The tips are pointed and the pad takes up a large

DEER

F2 h2

portion of the hoof. (Review the drawings of feet in Chapter 4.) While it is usually not possible to identify the pad in the print of the moose, it is often possible to identify the rounded depression left by the pad in the elk print. Dew claws often show in moose prints.

The round outline of the caribou hoof, the rounded tips, and the abundance of prints are enough to identify caribou tracks.

The sides of mountain sheep tracks are straight and the overall print is wedge-shaped. Look for the raised, half-moon-shaped center in the prints. The print of the mountain goat appears blocky and the tips are wider and more rounded than those of mountain sheep.

Although both animals may show dew claws, they are often absent. Where mountain sheep occur within the ranges of antelope, track identification can also be hard. Look for the rounded pads characteristic of antelope.

Muskox tracks are round with rounded tips. The overall outline is round but flattened lengthwise. Dew claws seldom show.

Bison tracks are very large and robust. Their overall outline is round, and on hard surfaces it is possible to confuse them with horse tracks. Look for the separation between the halves of the hoof. The tips of the hoof are pointed. Dew claws seldom show.

DEER ORDER

F2(4) h2(4)

Members	Front Length in	(cm)	Front Width in	(cm)	Hind Length in	(cm)	Hind Width in	(cm)	Walking Straddle in	(cm)
Antelope	2¾	(7)	2¼ −	(5)	2½	(6.4)	2 +	(5.2)	??	??
Peccary	1½	(3.7)	1½ −	(3.6)	1¼	(3.2)	1¼	(3.2)	4½	(11)
Deer										
White-tailed	3	(7.5)	1⅞	(4.8)	2⅝	(6.7)	1½	(3.8)	6	(15)
Mule	3¼	(8.3)	2⅝	(6.7)	3⅛	(7.9)	2½	(6.4)	6	(15)
Caribou	3½	(8.9)	3¾	(9.5)	3¼	(8.3)	3½	(8.9)	10	(25)
Elk	4¾	(12)	3	(7.5)	4¼	(11)	2⅞	(7.3)	8	(20)
Moose	6	(15)	3½	(8.9)	5⅝	(14)	3½	(8.9)	10	(25)
Mountain goat	3	(7.5)	1⅞	(4.8)	2⅝	(6.7)	1½	(3.8)	7	(18)
Bighorn sheep	3½	(8.9)	2½	(6.4)	3	(7.5)	2	(5.1)	7	(19)
Muskox	4⅜	(11)	5	(13)	4	(10)	5 −	(12)	10	(25)
Bison	6¼	(16)	6¾	(17)	6	(15)	6	(15)	??	??

A plus or minus indicates that the track averages slightly larger (+) or smaller (−) than the measurement.

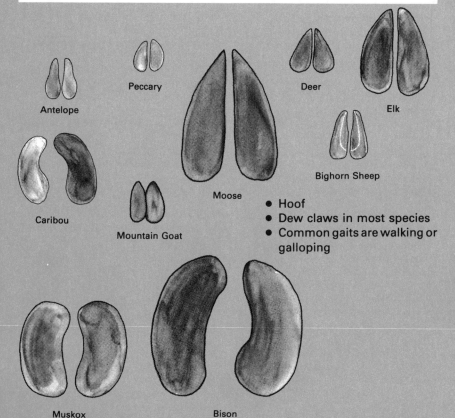

Antelope

Peccary

Deer

Elk

Bighorn Sheep

Caribou

Moose

Mountain Goat

Muskox

Bison

- Hoof
- Dew claws in most species
- Common gaits are walking or galloping

15. Reading Trails

Hidden in the trails of mammals are the stories of their lives. The mammals have written these stories carefully, and the stories are awaiting the nature detective who can successfully unravel the clues. Clues contain a wealth of information about character, mood, success at finding food, and even the mammal's sex life. Much of the fun in tracking is reading what the trails have to tell you. But learning to read these stories does not happen quickly. It takes practice to gain the necessary skills and insight.

I have provided this chapter to aid you in becoming a successful tracker. Here, based mostly on my slides and field notes, are many of the stories I have observed in the field. I would like to "walk" you through the tales that these trails have to tell.

This chapter has been designed to provide practice in interpreting clues and reading trails; it is a type of self-test. On the first page you will find a drawing of a real tracking situation. For each drawing, you will be asked to identify the mammal or mammals and for some situations you will be asked to decipher the story left in the tracks.

First, read the details that are given. Then analyze the clues. I suggest that you write the clues on a sheet of paper. As a guideline, I would suggest that you do not guess before you have identified at least four major clues. After you have assembled your clues, make your final judgement or interpretation of the story.

My goal in this chapter is to get you to think like a wild mammal!

Some hints:

- Check the surface and habitat.

- Determine the size of the tracks. (Look for scales.)
- Determine the size of the mammal. (Stride length when walking equals the hip to shoulder length.)
- Determine the speed at which the mammal was moving. (Foot length in reference to stride.)
- Look for clues that will identify the family or order.
- Consider relative size within the taxonomic group.
- Look for behavioral clues that tell a story.

At first the drawings may appear abstract and nonsensical. The clues may be indistinct and all the information you'd like not there. Indeed, this is often the situation in the field, but you must learn to decipher the information that you find. Don't be discouraged but look carefully. Pick a starting area and interpret the information there. Concentrate on your starting area until you understand it thoroughly. Then move on to other parts of the picture. As you understand small parts, try to form an image of the whole scene in your mind. Eventually the story will become clear.

On the second page you will find the interpretation that I made in the field. You may also be referred to one of the color behavioral drawings for further information. Check the story that I read against the story that you interpreted. You may then wish to go back and look at the drawing again.

Best of luck in this self-test. Go slowly, interpret carefully, and you will find some interesting tales.

Trail 1

Task: We'll start with an easy one. All you have to do with the first one is to identify the mammal.

Location: These tracks were observed on the edge of a dense coniferous forest on the Frying Pan River of central Colorado. The elevation was over 10,000 feet (3000 m).

Clues: The ruler is six inches (15 cm) and the surface is light, newly fallen snow.

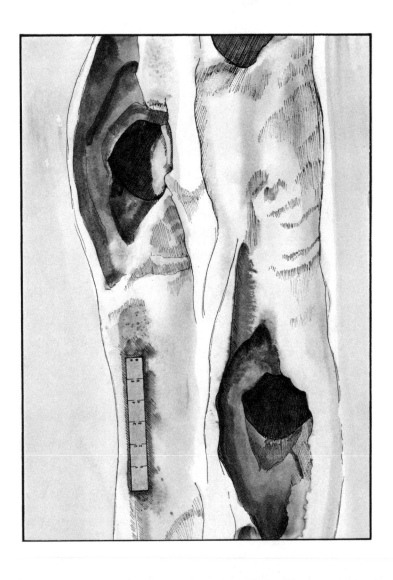

Identification: Canada lynx

Clues: The main part of each print is about four inches (10 cm) across and is wider than long. The lynx was walking (a single step is only about 12 inches [30 cm]), and the stride, which indicates hip to shoulder length, would be over 24 inches (60 cm).

The hair on the feet seems to have made the prints look larger and to hide individual toes. Look closely at the right print; there is a hint of four toes but no claws. Definite drag marks exist on both sides of the prints indicating a very hairy foot.

Even though there was light new snow the lynx did not sink in because of the larger surface of its feet. A mountain lion has the same size foot as the lynx, but it weighs over 100 pounds (45 kg), whereas the lynx does not weight over 40 pounds (18 kg).

Comments: The clues that told me this was a cat are the rounded prints (at least wider than long), no obvious claws, and to a certain extent the fact that it was walking. The lion was ruled out because the tracks did not sink deep enough and the stride was so short. The hairy foot is suggestive of a mammal that evolved for winter conditions or in the far north. A forested habitat at high mountain altitudes further supported this conclusion. All clues considered, the trail was that of a walking lynx.

Trail 2

Task: This time you must identify the animal and tell the story. It is a short story but poignant in the reality it reveals about the arid west.

Location: This story was observed near Poison Spider, west of Casper, Wyoming. The site is on the edge of the Red Desert.

Clues: The July night before I happened on the tracks, there had been a thunderstorm which left small puddles on the dirt road. By noon, the water had just evaporated, but there was still a surface of fine wet mud. In another hour, the mud would have dried out. The scale is six inches (15 cm).

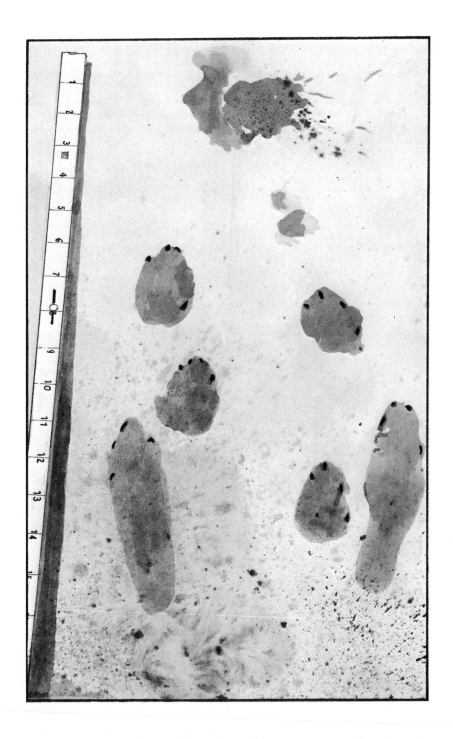

Identification: The large hind feet identified this as a hopping mammal. Four toes are evident in both the front and hind feet, indicating that this is a rabbit. The relatively small size of the feet gave the prints away as cottontail.

Comments: During the early morning hours, the rabbit hopped slowly up to the edge of the remaining water. It then sat on its hind feet and slowly stretched its body out to the water by moving its front feet forward one at a time. A deeper depression is seen where the tongue of the cottontail lapped at the water and some of the mud was even dislodged to the left. What a treat even this muddy water must be to the desert mammals!

Trail 3

Task: Identify the mammal.

Location: This trail was observed one morning east of Boulder, Colorado, at Sawhill Ponds in the flood plain of Boulder Creek.

Clues: There was about 3/4 inch (2 cm) of snow on top of a frozen pond. The comb is five inches (12.7 cm) long.

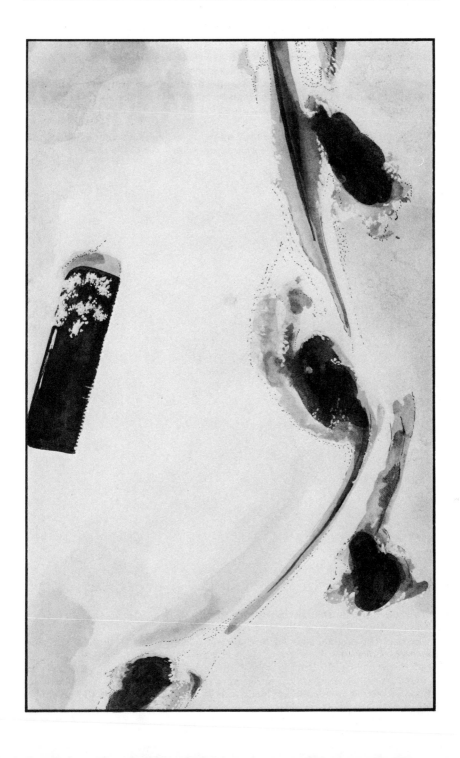

Identification: Muskrat

Clues: The prints are not clear enough to ascertain the number of toes. The animal appears to be a sloppy walker as it waddles along. Notice the drag marks into each print. Certainly it was not moving fast as the distance between prints is about the length of the prints. Hip-shoulder length is less than 15 inches (38 cm). The mammal was dragging a narrow, hairless tail.

Comments: The drag mark is judged to be its tail because mammals that are carrying prey items usually leave a drag mark to one side of the tracks.

Trail 4

Task: Identify the animals and tell the story.

Location: The original slide for this tale was taken by Bob Rozinski at Chatfield Reservoir, Colorado.

Clues: The grasslands were covered by a couple inches (about 5 cm) of snow. Although there is no readily apparent scale in the picture, you should be able to judge size by the blades of grass sticking through the snow.

Identification: Ground squirrel and a raptor.

Clues: Two trails led from the hole in the upper right corner. These trails showed a 2x bounding pattern which was perpendicular to the line of travel. There were drag marks leading into and out of the print patterns. On the edges of the large disturbed area on the left, imprints of bird feathers were observed. In the lower left corner, pieces of the squirrel's body and fur were found.

Comments: The ground squirrel had been traveling in and out of its hole. On the last time as it neared the hole, a raptor hit it and dragged it fighting into the snow. The inclination of the feather imprints indicates that the raptor came from the direction of the top of the page. The raptor was not able to finish all of its meal before Bob happened upon the scene.

Trail 5

Task: Identify the mammal.

Location: This trail was observed near Heart Lake in Yellowstone National Park.

Clues: Although the snow was deep, it was somewhat heavy and therefore solid. No scale is presented here, but if you think about it for a while, you won't need the scale.

Identification: Porcupine

Clues: The porcupine was walking because the distance between steps is no longer than the length of the foot. Although there is no scale, a small mammal had to have made this track. Think for a minute about a bear. If these were bear tracks there would be no way that the tracks could be so close together; the hip-shoulder length would be too great.

Obviously this animal was not in a hurry, indicated by the short steps and the tendency for the prints to be toed-in.

Drag marks are present, swinging in from the right side. The porcupine sank fairly deep into the snow because of its weight and small feet.

Comments: The story I read here was that of a slow-moving animal that normally did not hurry. If you are pigeon-toed, you can't hurry. Try walking pigeon-toed and see if you can move very fast. What sort of mammal would not hurry? One that has ample defenses against predators. Thus the heavy drag marks of the tail. The tail, of course, was weighted down with protection—the load of quills.

Trail 6

Task: Identify the mammal and tell the story.

Location: This story was observed at West Thumb, Yellowstone. The tracks were on the ice of Yellowstone Lake.

Clues: There were about two inches (5 cm) of heavy snow on top of the ice. My boot prints are about 11 inches (28 cm) long.

Identification: River otter

Clues: The 2x bounding pattern is that of the weasel family. Individual prints are relatively large, which ruled out the weasel and marten. Because it was winter, skunks would have been hibernating. A tail drag mark was present beside the 2x bound pattern. The long sliding trail was the clincher that identified this trail as that of the playful river otter.

Comments: First the otter crossed the picture from the right to the left. It was moving rapidly as shown by the 2x pattern (the large otters usually use a 1-2-1x loping gait). When it returned from the left side, it planted all four feet and dove forward to slide on its stomach with its front feet held close to its sides. At the end of its slide, the otter continued on its way using a 2x bounding gait.

Trail 7

Task: Identify the mammal and explain what it was doing.

Location: The original photo was taken near South Pass, Wyoming, near the edge of the Red Desert.

Clues: Rocky ledges are common and this set of tracks was observed on a slight rise overlooking the surrounding valley. The habitat was mostly grassland, although a few conifers could be found in moister areas. A couple of inches (5 cm) of snow were on the ground. The comb is five inches (12.7 cm) long.

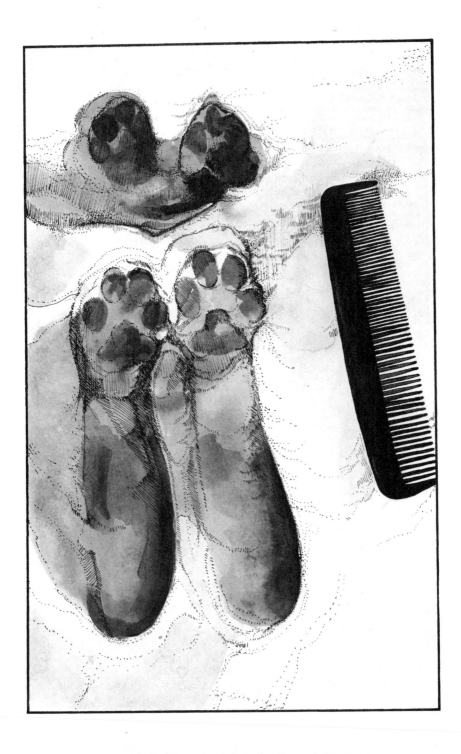

Identification: Bobcat

Clues: No claws are present in the clearer upper print. The intermediate pad is bilobed on the front margin. The prints appear longer than wide, which is not indicative of cats. However, the shape in this case is a product of what the animal was doing. Note also the depression in front of the clear tracks and the long depression connecting to the heels of the hind prints.

Comments: Bobcats are not inclined to make long chases for animals. Therefore, this bobcat had gone to the top of the ridge to survey the valley. At the top, it sat for a while and watched. The sitting motion caused the upper portions of the hind legs to register. Sitting and then getting up put a longtitudinal stress on the hind feet and caused longer than normal prints. The front feet, which were moved during this process, did not register clearly.

Trail 8

Task: Identify the animals.

Location: Near Shoshone Geyser Basin, Yellowstone National Park.

Clues: The area was in a lodgepole pine forest with six feet of snow (2 m). The picture was taken in January 1974. The comb is five inches (12.7 cm) long.

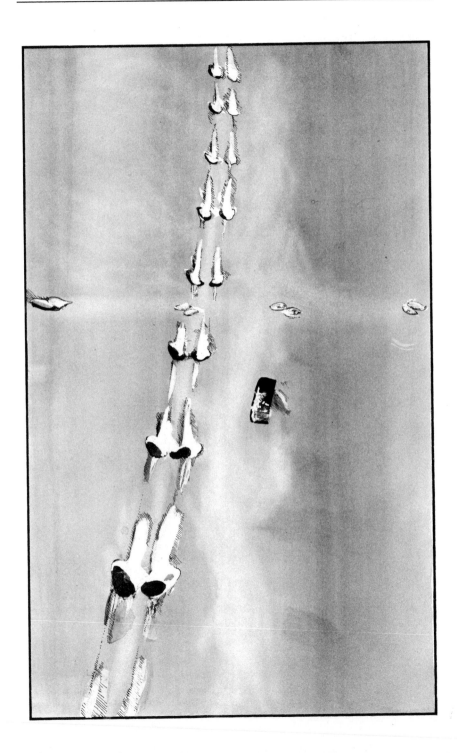

Identification: A chickaree (tree squirrel) crossed from bottom to top, and an ermine crossed from left to right.

Clues: The squirrel was identified by the paired prints which are perpendicular to the line of travel. Drag marks leading into and out of the prints are also visible. The weasel was identified by the prints placed diagonally to the line of travel.

Comments: The weasel did not sink nearly as deep into the snow as did the chickaree, and the tracks are much smaller. On the basis of size, the tracks must have been from the smaller of the two weasels present in Yellowstone, the ermine. Since the tracks are so small, I would even guess that this was a female. Young are not born until May, and the young from last year would have been full-grown in January.

Trail 9

Task: Identify the animal. Be careful—this is a hard one. Analyze all the clues carefully. As a hint, remember the technique of elimination.

Location: The original slide was taken by Tass Kelso at the University of Colorado Mountain Research Station west of Boulder, Colorado.

Clues: The altitude was 10,000 feet (3,030 m) and the habitat was dense lodgepole pine forest. The snowpack was hard due to wind packing. The lens cap in the center is just under two inches in diameter (5 cm).

Identification: Snowshoe hare

Clues: Four toes are present in all clear prints. The spacing between toes is equal. The plantar pad is symmetrical and hollow at the base. The hare was milling around and not passing straight through.

Comments: These prints seem to have clues from several families. Therefore, it was helpful to go through a mental list of families and check off those that it couldn't be. My thinking process went like this. Dog family—no, because claws did not show and plantar pads were hollow. Cat family—no, because the plantar pads were hollow and not bilobed. Weasel family—no, because there were too few toes and no 1-3-1 spacing was present. Bear family—no way, and the same for the raccoon family. Well, then what? Rodents—no, because the fifth toe was lacking. Rabbit family—well, hmmmm, maybe. Certainly no clues ruled out rabbits. However, generally rabbits show a heel print. But the heel imprint is due to hopping. When rabbits walk they are up on their toes and a heel imprint does not show.

If you spend a lot of time tracking during the winter and follow rabbit tracks, you will occasionally see walking tracks. Although rabbits do not walk for great distances, the tracks can easily be confused with those from the dog and cat families.

Trail 10

Task: Identify the mammals.

Location: These tracks were observed near the Colorado River east of Moab, Utah.

Clues: The tracks were on a mud flat below a recent high water line. The mud was very moist and tracks were easily recorded. It was the sort of mud that you dread crossing in your shoes. The scale is six inches (15 cm).

Identification: A beaver crossed from right to left, and a gray fox crossed from top to bottom.

Clues: The large hind foot with webbing identifies the beaver. The gray fox tracks may be identified by their longer-than-wide shape, one lobe on the plantar pad, and occasional claw prints.

Comments: The gray fox is the only canid that can climb trees by using its claws. It is also a very light-weight mammal. Therefore, it is not surprising that the semi-retractile claws fail to show in the mud. Because the animal is so light, the outside edges of the plantar pads on the hind feet fail to register. The resulting pad appears as a round depression. I have also observed this trait in the hind prints of coyotes.

The hind feet of the beaver are readily identified. However, there is one print at the center of the bottom which may be confusing. Since four toes register, it might be identified as a cat or dog. The print is actually the front foot of the beaver. It appears deep because the beaver is heavy in relationship to the small area of the front foot. Part of another front print can be seen under the hind print above. Notice the slight toed-in stance.

Trail 11

Task: Identify the mammal and tell a story.

Location: The original slide was shot by Dave Slovisky in Canyonlands National Park.

Clues: The surface is soft sand and the scale is six inches (15 cm).

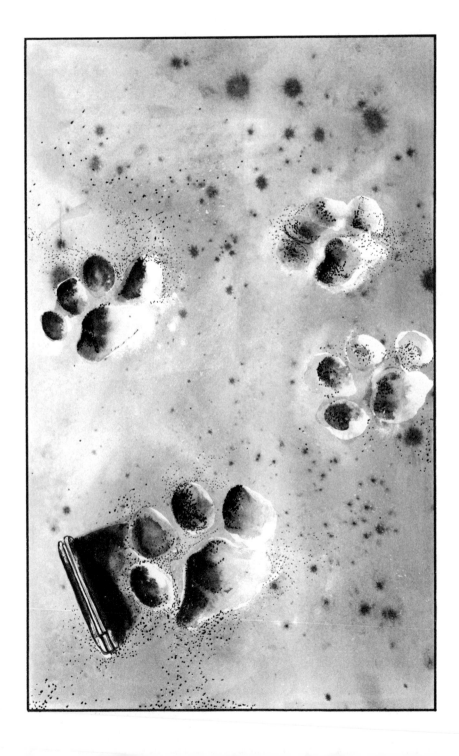

Identification: Mountain lion

Clues: Tracks appeared roundish, wider than long. Four toes were present but no claws were observed. The bilobing on the plantar pad was not present because the great weight of the lion flattened the impression in the soft sand.

Comments: Careful inspection shows that the two tracks to the left are smaller than the other two. A mother lion walked past this point with her cub. The cub's tracks are less distinct, giving an impression that the tracks are possibly older. However, this is because the cub's light weight did not make a deep impression.

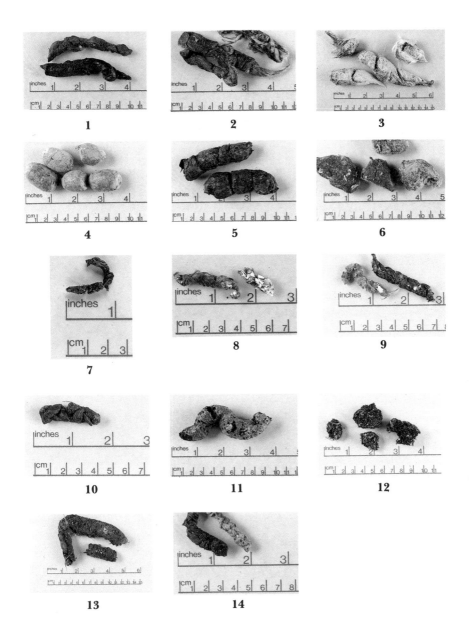

15

16

17

18

19

20

21

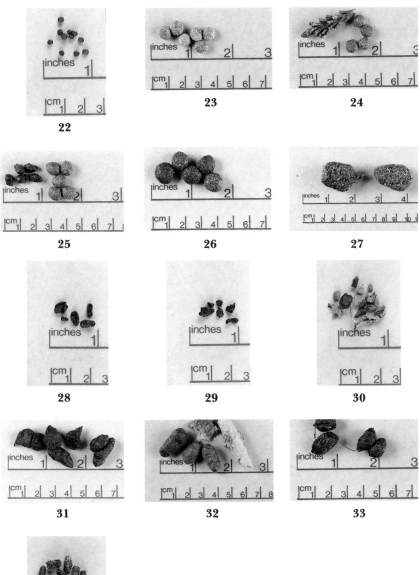

22

23

24

25

26

27

28

29

30

31

32

33

34

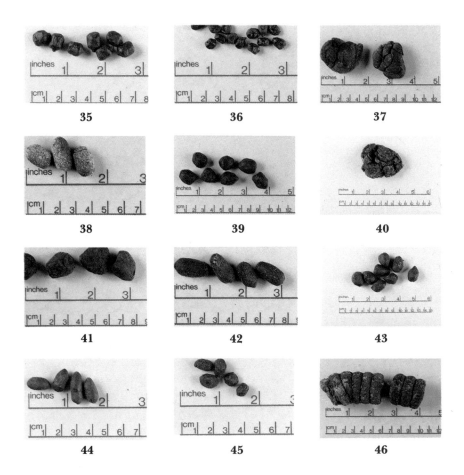

35

36

37

38

39

40

41

42

43

44

45

46

SCAT PHOTOGRAPHS

Color photographs have been provided to illustrate the great variation in scats. In order to show detail, within the scat, we took close-up photographs of a portion of the cords of a scat pile or of a few pellets of a clump. Remember, when observing, that the total quantity of scat is a good relative indicator of species size within a group.

For ease of comparison, all photographs were taken against the same background and scale. The white fibers you will occasionally see stuck to the scat in the photographs are cotton packing material.

Abbreviations for sources of specimens: MC for Murie Collection, Teton Science School; 1/2c for the author's material; YNP for Yellowstone National Park; CNP for Canyonlands National Park; DNP for Denali National Park; RMNP for Rocky National Park; GSD for Great Sand Dunes National Monument; JH for Jackson Hole; ACES for Aspen Center of Environmental Sciences; TSS for Teton Science School; NR for Niwot Ridge; and MRS for the Mountain Research Station. Both NR and MRS are located west of Boulder, Colorado. The photography is by Tom Schenck, Camren, Inc.

1. Red Fox. The lower scat contains mostly by-products of the digestion of animal protein; the upper scat contains more hair and is lighter in color. (Sawhill ponds, Boulder, CO, 1/2c)

2. Coyote. The upper scat contains vegetable material; blades of grass are obvious. The lower scat contains mostly deer hair, but the darkness in the center indicates that some meat was left on the carcass. (NR, 1/2c)

3. Wolf. This scat is composed entirely of caribou hair, indicating that there was not much meat left on the carcass. (DNP, MC)

4. Bobcat. Definite segments identify this cat scat. Scat from drier regions is more segmented than that from non-desert areas. (Sheldon Range, NV, MC)

5. Lynx. Segmentation identifies this as cat scat, and the dark color indicates that the lynx was eating an animal protein diet. (DNP, MC)

6. Mountain Lion. A large portion of this scat is deer hair, but some animal protein is present. The number of bone fragments indicates that the lion ate several bones. Perhaps this scat represents the final remnants of a carcass. (Rabbit Ears Pass, CO, 1/2c)

7. Weasel. This scat from a small weasel is composed of hair and animal protein. (MRS, 1/2c)

8. Mink. The scat on the right contains numerous pieces of crayfish exoskeleton, while the one on the left contains fur, possibly that of a jumping mouse. (RMNP, 1/2c)

9. Mink. The scat on the right contains fish scales and animal protein; that on the left contains fur, possibly that of a muskrat. (RMNP, 1/2c)

10. Marten. This scat is composed of animal protein and is formed into looped cords. (MRS, 1/2c)

11. Striped Skunk. The scat is fairly large in diameter and must be from a large animal. The silverish color is due to varnish. The black in the lower left corner is the true color. (Elk Refuge, JH, WY, MC)

12. River Otter. Composed of fish scales, this scat is very fragile. Individual scales and vertebrae reflect light in the photograph. (JH, WY, 1/2c)

13. Raccoon. The omnivorous diet of the raccoon is shown by this coarse scat containing animal protein, bits of bones, and vegetation. (ACES, CO, 1/2c)

14. Ringtail. The scat on the left is mostly animal protein; the one on the right is composed of vegetable matter. (Nevada?, MC)

15. Black Bear. The scat is composed entirely of grass. (YNP, 1/2c)

16. Black Bear. The bear was feeding on a fresh elk carcass and the scat is mostly animal protein. The few pieces of vegetation in the scat may have been in the stomach or intestinal track of the elk. (Gros Ventre Mtns., WY, 1/2c)

17. Black Bear. Seeds of pin cherry and snowberry are present in this fragile and easily broken scat. (MRS, 1/2c)

18. Black Bear. The woody fragments are acorn shells. (Sangre De Cristo mountains near GSD, 1/2c)

19. Grizzly Bear. The woody fragments are pine nuts. (YNP, MC)

20. Grizzly Bear. Diameter is about 2½ in (6.4 cm). (YNP, MC)

21. Grizzly Bear. The slight blue tint in this scat indicates a diet of blueberries. Blueberry leaves are also visible. (Glacier National Park, 1/2c)

22. Pika. Round pellets characterize the rabbit order. (NR, 1/2c)

23. Cottontail Rabbit. The faint green color indicates moist vegetation; plant fragments are visible. (CNP, 1/2c)

24. Cottontail Rabbit. After the early snows, cottontails were feeding on lodgepole pine twigs. Scat and twig tips were present under low hanging branches. (MRS, 1/2c)

25. Snowshow Hare. The black pellets on the left are the nutrient-rich pellets that rabbits re-ingest. The other pellets are the ones usually found. (MRS, 1/2c)

26. Jackrabbit. Scat from the white-tailed jackrabbit were obtained near Rand, CO. (1/2c)

27. Beaver. These scats are composed mostly of coarse woody chips. (Snake River, JH, WY, MC)

28. Chickaree (Pine Squirrel). The soft, amorphous pellets indicate a moist diet. (MRS, 1/2c)

29. Golden-mantled Ground Squirrel. Soft, amorphous squirrel pellets indicate a moist diet. (MRS, 1/2c)

30. Chickaree. Additional signs, including pine cone scales and pieces of twigs, were found with this scat. The whiter pellets have been attacked by fungus. The three dark pellets in center are the natural color. (MRS, 1/2c)

31. Marmot. Marmots usually produce dark amorphous pellets that are much larger than those of the rest of the squirrels. These may look like marten scats, but the presence of many scats at a latrine indicates marmots. (NR, 1/2c)

32. Porcupine. Porcupines produce red-colored pellets during the winter when they are feeding mostly on conifers. (Mt. Evans, CO, 1/2c)

33. Porcupine. Porcupines produce black or dark pellets during the summer when they feed mostly on grasses, herbs, and shrubs. (MRS, 1/2c)

34. Pocket Gopher. Woody material and grass blades are present in these gopher scats. (*Thomomys talpoides*, NR, 1/2c)

35. Mule Deer. The nipple-dimple shape, more often associated with elk pellets, is apparent. (Teton National Forest, 1/2c). See also antelope scat.

36. Mule Deer. These small pellets came from a known-age, 18-month old deer. They are smaller than those of an adult deer. (ACES, CO, 1/2c)

37. Mule Deer. These pellets were very soft because of a moist spring diet. After they were deposited, they dried and bleached to a light brown. (CNP, 1/2c)

38. Mule Deer. The deer that produced these pellets was eating on a dry woody diet. The pellets, although small, resemble moose pellets. (CNP, 1/2c)

39. Elk. The nipple-dimple shape is apparent on these pellets, but the nipple end is rounded. The scat were produced on August 22, 1979 when the vegetation had started to dry out. (NR, 1/2c)

40. Elk. A moist diet in the spring formed soft pellets that stuck together in this large clump. (NR, 1/2c)

41. Elk. Large elk scat produced in July on a moist diet. (YNP, 1/2c)

42. Moose. These pellets were from a yearling moose browsing on woody vegetation. In color and shape, they are the same as those produced by adults, but they are smaller. (YNP, 1/2c)

43. Moose. Pellets produced from a moist diet of stream vegetation in October. (TSS, WY, 1/2c)

44. Antelope. These scats, produced in the winter, are longer than usual. I have also noticed the tendency for mule deer scats produced during winter to be longer than those produced the rest of the year. (Near Walden, CO, 1/2c)

45. Big Horn Sheep. A dry early June diet produced these separate pellets. (Mt. Evans, CO, 1/2c)

46. Buffalo. A calf, grazing on dry feed, produced this hard, layered scat. Its small size is due to the small size of the calf. (YNP, 1/2c)

16. Scatology

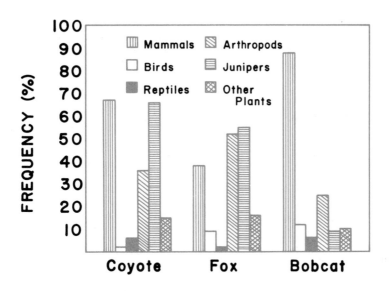

Scat analysis shows that coyotes, foxes, and bobcats in Arizona use different portions of the available resources. Coyotes and bobcats are more carnivorous and foxes are more insectivorous. Both canids eat a considerable amount of vegetation. Figures represent the percentage of the scat containing a certain item (after Turkowski, 1980). Since a scat may contain more than one item, percentages total more than 100%.

Scat, the feces of mammals, provides you, the naturalist, an important window into the mammalian world. Information we gather from scat includes mammal identification and presence, location of activities, composition of diet, seasonal diet changes, and samples of prey species. The scientific study of scat, **scatology**, once solely the realm of the naturalist, has grown into a valuable tool for ecological research.

Since 1970 the number of scientific studies of scat has increased dramatically. As scatology evolved from the descriptive stage, exemplified by Murie's work, many new and innovative techniques were utilized for species identification. Starting in the 1960s, the pH of scat (a measure of acidity) has

been used to identify species and even as an indicator of food items in the diet. The technique has been used successfully with herbivores, including deer, elk, goats, porcupine, and sheep. However, little success has been obtained with predators. **Bile acids** in scat have been used to identify species whose scat is visually hard to distinguish. This technique has been helpful in working with carnivores. The presence of host-specific internal **parasites** in scat identifies some carnivores. Scat **size differences** in canines have received attention since 1979. Most recently, differences in the amount of the **protein** albumin have been used to separate deer species.

Many studies are now available that

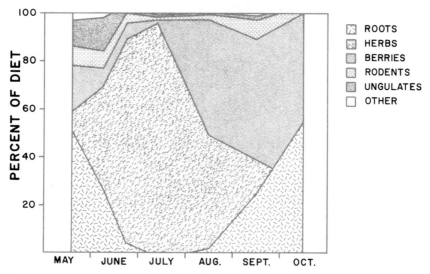

The composition of scat shows what grizzlies eat in Denali National Park. The diet changes dramatically during the non-hibernating season and is mostly herbaceous material (after Murie, 1981).

analyze diet and seasonal diet changes for herbivores and carnivores. Diet analysis techniques have been perfected, and many studies have been made to calibrate the accuracy of the methods. The use of scat gives us insights into nutritional needs of mammals without harming them.

Size

A by-product of scatological research has been a great appreciation of the variability inherent in scat and the difficulties naturalists have in identifying scat. It has proven difficult to identify carnivore species from their scat. For example, the scat of fox, coyote, wolf, bobcat, lion, and badger can easily be confused with one or more other species. Experience has shown that visual identification of scat without additional clues may be correct only 50 to 66% of the time. Experienced naturalists in laboratory tests of unmarked scat correctly identified only 88% of lion scat and 64% of bobcat scat. The wrong identifications stress the need for other supporting clues, including tracks, whenever

possible. Remember the principle of positive verification mentioned in the tracking section, and whenever possible verify the origin of scat.

Size has always been a prime criterion for scat identification, and many naturalists have positively stated, on the basis of size, that a scat was deposited by a coyote, for example. To illustrate size variation, I have assembled information from three studies on the diameters of canine feces. The size distributions were derived from 1,440 positively identified scats as follows: 95 gray fox, 129 red fox, 926 coyote, and 290 wolf. All four species produce scats in the range of 13 to 20 mm. No single diameter will positively separate these species. Any single diameter used as a criterion to separate two species will misidentify a certain percentage of the scat.

On the basis of the graph, you can define criteria to best suit the goals of your study. For the general naturalist, I suggest that scats less than 18 mm could be considered fox, those 18 mm to 25 mm could be considered coyote, and those 25 mm or larger could be considered wolf. Using these criteria,

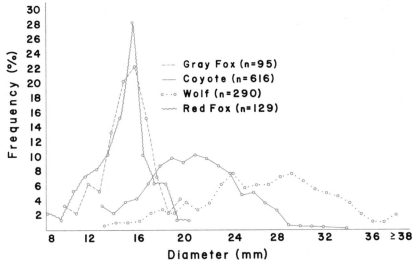

Considerable overlap exists in the size of canid scat. While the diameter ranges from 8 to greater than 38 mm (1.5 in), gray foxes, red foxes, coyotes, and wolves all produce scat in the range of 13 to 20 mm. Data are from Dannner and Dodd (1982), Green and Flinders (1981), and Weaver and Fritts (1979).

the percentages of correctly identified scats would be:

Species (criteria)	Percent Correct
Fox (less than 18 mm)	
Gray Fox	89%
Red Fox	92%
Coyote (18 to less than 25 mm)	63%
(*18.5% are less than 18 mm)	
Wolf (25 mm or larger)	63%
(*4.55% are less than 18 mm)	

* These would be classified as fox scats on the basis of the 18-mm criterion.

METHODS

Collections

Permanent, verified collections of scat serve as valuable references for the naturalist. The collections allow us to correctly identify unknown field specimens and, if extensive enough, also show the amount of variability within a species. If you properly label and display your collections, they may also serve as an educational tool for teaching classes and for others to study. I find that my collections are in constant demand because a verified scat collection is a rare commodity in any part of the country. Many naturalists desire the knowledge available from a collection, but a few have had the time to actually make a complete collection.

When making the initial scat collections in the field, you should collect enough material to show the variation within a particular scat deposition. You do not need to collect all of the scat. However, extra amounts can be used as trading material with other naturalists. If possible take a photograph with a scale to show the actual quantity of scat deposited, its location, and the habitat. Take a good set of field notes recording all facts that might be significant.

In the field, I use Ziploc™ plastic bags and 3x5 inch (7.6 x 12.7 cm) file cards. Ziploc™ bags provide a quick seal-proof method of collecting even wetter scat. A file card can be labeled and dropped into the bag. While you are in the field be careful not to smash the scat. You can buy light-weight, cheap plastic boxes, or food storage containers can be purchased at supermarkets. These boxes can be carried in your pack to provide a rigid container to protect your collections.

You must take scat out of the plastic as soon as possible; otherwise the scat will become moldy. Upon returning from the field, remove the scat and put it and the label card in the center of a piece of **newspaper**. Double the newspaper and fold the edges over to seal the package. Staple the folded edges shut. Finally, use a black marking pen to label the paper with a date. The newspaper is porous, and the scat can dry inside the paper envelope. These packages can then be dried in an out-of-the-way place such as in an outside garage. If a convenient place is not available, make a drying box. You can make a simple one from 1/4 inch (0.6 cm) wire mesh from a hardware store. Fold the mesh into a box and wire the edges closed. Once the scat is inside, wire the top shut. If the drying box is stored outside, it will keep animals from getting into the scat. The drying box can be attached to a tree, but you must shelter it so rain or snow does not get on the scat. The box will work in the summer and winter. Freezing will not hurt the scat. Drying time will depend on the wetness of the scat and the relative humidity.

Dried scat has relatively little odor and is somewhat resistant to damage from handling. However, you may wish to seal it with a protective coating to prevent it from falling apart in the future. Providing a protective cover for more fragile types of scat, such as river otter, is important if your collection is to last. I have had success with clear **varnish**. More recently, I have been working with spray-on **plastic**. The brand I have used is Krylon™ (No. 1303—Crystal Clear). Coating the scat may be more important in wetter climates where mildew is more prevalent.

You should first test the material you are using as a coating. Paint the varnish onto a few pieces of scat and let it dry. Then compare the coated scat to the original to see if the color remains true.

When you buy varnish, ask the dealer for a brand that will not yellow with age. Once you have tested and are happy with your coating, use it to cover all the scat you wish to preserve.

Store your scat collection so that is is easily visible. Clear plastic **"fishing boxes"** that can be purchased at most variety and discount stores work well. These boxes are relatively cheap, and a choice of sizes is available. You can customize the boxes by removing their plastic partitions. I use two sizes of boxes: one for large scat and one for smaller scat. Using only two sizes allows for more convenient storing. Place a soft surface in the bottom of each compartment. This can be cotton or plastic bubble or styrofoam packing. The boxes will scratch each other when you stack them, so separate them from each other with softer material. Scat can also be stored and displayed in **Riker Mounts** available at BioQuip Products, 1320 E. Franklin Ave., El Segundo, CA 90245.

Around the house and for traveling between classes, I keep my natural history collections, including scat, in cardboard file boxes. These are available from discount stores and offer a convenient method of storage.

Photographs also provide an excellent method of documenting scat. First take a photograph that shows the scat in its natural setting. Try to include any scratchings made by the mammal. When possible take the photograph in the sunlight. You can use a mirror (or aluminum foil on cardboard) as a reflector to provide better light to all sides. If the scat is located in the shade, a flash is very useful. I also carry a **neutral gray card** by Kodak. Photographing the scat on this card provides me with a uniform background so that I can better compare scat colors.

Determining Age

In general, scat becomes drier and harder with age; the moister the scat, the fresher it is. However, rain or snow can make scat appear fresher than it really is. Really fresh scat will still be steaming, it will be warmer than the surrounding environment and you can detect warmth by feeling with your fingers. The rate at which scat stops steaming and cools off will depend on the air temperature. As a tracker you must keep the recent weather in mind.

When scat of either carnivores or herbivores is moist, insects provide clues for aging. When scat is first deposited, you may see flies laying eggs on it. Eggs are present for only a few days. The hatching of eggs into larvae signals that the scat is several days old

Diet Analyses

The analysis of scat composition can be used to determine the **diets** of mammals, what they were grazing or preying on. Sophisticated techniques have been developed to make realistic estimates of the number and **biomass** (weight of animals) of prey species eaten.

The basic technique for fecal analysis is **fractionation** of scat to find items that you can recognize. **Recognition items** are identified to species, and an estimate is made of the number of each species eaten. With carnivores, identification is based on bones, teeth, hair, and feathers; with herbivores, identification is made from plant parts, which are usually microscopic in size. Identification is aided by the possession of a permanent reference collection of food items including material on prepared

microscope slides. Quantification in diet analysis is complicated by differences in digestibility of various food items—some parts digest easily and others don't.

You can make simple diet analyses of carnivore scat by picking the scat apart and identifying major items. With a little preparation, you can do more complicated analyses. First wash the scat using a low-sudsing detergent, to remove odoriferous and water soluble materials. Some researchers place scat in nylon bags and use automatic washing machines for this procedure, but you can wash scat in a bowl in the sink. Rinse the scat thoroughly. If the scat is still intact, place it in water in a small bowl to float off the remaining hair. The process can be speeded up by using toothpicks to break up (fractionate) the scat. Separate food items into piles: sand, plant materials, seeds, bones, scales, feathers, hair, teeth, and insect parts. Finally, dry the materials to bring out their colors.

Initial procedures for washing and separating material from herbivore scat are similar to those for carnivore scat. However, because of the smaller plant parts, you will need to do much of the work with a microscope. A reference collection of plant parts is also necessary.

Once you have sorted the material, data can be summarized to show the frequency of occurrence (percent) of items in the animal's diet. For example, the frequency of prey in gray fox scat from Arizona shows seasonal preference (table). Gray foxes take rodents and in-

Seasonal comparison of food items in the diet of gray foxes. Values are percent of scat containing the items.

	Rabbit	Rodents	Hoofed Mammals	Birds	Reptiles	Juniper Arthropods	Other Berries	Other
Winter	0	16	10	0	0	11	90	5
Spring	3	27	0	3	3	47	74	3
Summer	4	33	17	21	4	88	13	25
Fall	0	39	4	13	0	57	44	35

More than one species and more than one item may occur in a scat; therefore, percentages may total higher than 100%. (After Turkowski, 1980.)

sects all year, with insects high in spring, summer, and fall. During the fall and winter, reptiles are absent from the diet, and hoofed mammals (probably in the form of carrion) are important, as are juniper berries that are available during the non-growing season. During the summer, birds become more important with the increased availability of nestlings. Plant material is also used heavily during summer and fall.

You can calculate absolute amounts eaten by adjusting for differential digestibility of prey items and then multiplying by the mean estimated weight of the prey items. Smaller prey items tend to be underestimated and large items overestimated. For coyotes, the correction factors for differences in digestion were developed by Weaver and Hoffman. You can see how they calculated prey numbers and biomass in coyote diets in the accompanying charts (below).

Precautions

It is possible for you to pick up an infectious disease from scat. However, this is not very likely, especially if you follow hygienic methods. When handling scat, avoid placing your hands around your eyes and mouth. Wash your hands when finished. For particularily fresh or wet scat, I often invert a Ziploc™ bag over my hand, pick up the scat, and re-invert the bag over it. Some people use plastic gloves, but I have never bothered. However, plastic gloves might be advisable if you are working with a group of young students. Freezing kills certain disease organisms found in scat, so storing scat at below freezing temperatures outside while drying it may have an additional benefit. Coating the scat also offers some protection.

If you should become ill when, or recently after, working with scat, visit your doctor and let him or her know that you have been working with scat. Once alerted, the doctor will be better prepared to diagnose uncommon diseases. Having provided this warning, I must say that I have never known a naturalist to pick up a disease from scat. However, good hygiene is always called for.

CHARACTERISTICS

Shape will help you separate the scat of herbivores from that of carnivores; herbivores produce scat that consists of

Diet analysis for coyote scat. It is assumed that ten prey items were detected in each case.

Prey Item	Number detected	Calibration*	Estimated of prey weight (g)	Number of prey consumed	Biomass consumed (g)
Pocket Mice	10	5.0	18	50	900
Deer Mice	10	4.6	19	46	874
Voles	10	2.9	25	29	725
Kangaroo Rat	10	1.5	50	15	750
Ground Squirrel (juvenile)	10	0.9	128	9	1152
Ground Squirrel (adult)	10	0.7	327	7	2289

*Calibration = A calibration factor developed from feeding experiements under laboratory conditions. Since one prey item may be defecated in more than one scat, the quantity of prey may be slightly overestimated. (After Weaver and Hoffman, 1979.)

small roundish pellets, while carnivores produce larger, cylindrical scats often with tapered ends. Shape and size will help us identify taxonomic orders—for example, distinguishing rodents from rabbits. However, the variability inherent in scat often makes it impossible to positively identify the species from which it came. Sometimes, we cannot identify the genus or the family. Since our classification of scat to species is tentative, we need supporting evidence whenever possible. Scat, once we have identified it to the species, provides us with valuable information.

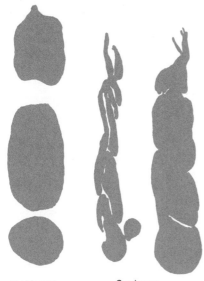

Herbivores   Carnivores
Examples of different types of droppings.

Below, I will discuss the characteristics of scat and explain what those characteristics tell us about the origin of the scat, the season of deposition, the feeding habits, and other activities of the mammals.

Types

Many mammals, including some shrews, rodents, and lagomorphs, produce two types of scat. The normal and more often observed scat is dry and dull

in color. The other type is dark in color and soft to semi-liquid in composition. The second type, which is produced at a much lower frequency, is rich in vitamins, especially those of the B-complex. The vitamins are a product of bacterial digestion within the intestine. Mammals re-ingest this dark scat for its nutritional value. This process is known as **coprophagy**. Coprophagy allows the animals to more completely utilize their natural diet. Because of coprophagy, the nutritionally-rich dark scat is hard to find. Occasionally, it will be observed in winter snows or during the spring meltout.

Texture

The texture of scat is dependent on the **moisture content** of the diet. Dry diets produce hard scat, often with separate pellets; wet diets produce soft or even runny scat, like "cow-pies." Moisture in the diet is dependent on season and food items. In the spring and early summer when the vegetation is young and growing rapidly, the moisture content is high. During this period, scat will be very soft, and mammals such as sheep and elk may produce very soft scat in which separate pellets may not be distinguishable. Late in the summer and fall, the vegetation becomes dry and the scat becomes harder.

The relative ratio of browsing to grazing influences moisture content. Increased amounts of browse (shrub and tree branches and conifer needles) produce harder scat. Grazing of grasses and herbs will produce softer scat. Carnivores feeding on flesh will produce softer scat. Carnivore diets that include more hair and bones will produce hard scat.

Often mammals will try to obtain nutrients from natural salt licks. In the process, they ingest sands and clay. Scat containing these materials will be very hard and dry. Scat containing large amounts of clay is in the form of rock-hard pellets.

Shape

Shape provides excellent clues to identification, especially at the order level. Basic forms include spheres, elongate spheres, cords, tails and clumps.

Spheres or slightly flattened spheres are characteristic of lagomorphs. The size continuum varies from the matchhead-sized pellets of pikas up to the marble-sized pellets of jackrabbits. Moist, softer pellets found during the summer may have a slight point at one end.

Elongate spheres (two to four times longer than wide) are found in the artiodactyla order. There is a tendency for these pellets to exhibit what I call the nipple-dimple shape. The protruding end (nipple) of one pellet fits into the dimple of the next pellet. The nipple-dimple is most developed in elk scat and can be used as a clue to separate elk from moose pellets, which are shaped like robin eggs.

Cords are many times longer than wide and are characteristic of the carnivores. Four types may be recognized: thin, thick, broken, and looped. Thin cords belong not to mammals but to the birds. I mention them here because the thin cords are often mistaken for mammal scat. The most confusing thin cords are usually produced by ducks, geese, grouse, and ptarmigans.

Thick cords, which are relatively thicker in reference to their length, characterize the larger carnivores including dogs, bears, and raccoons. A thick cord generally forms a single longer cord that does not fold back on itself.

A broken cord is characteristic of the cat family. It is robust enough to be recognized as a thick cord but has a tendency to be constricted or segmented. The distance between constrictions is equal to or slightly larger than the width of the scat. The drier the habitat, the greater the tendency for segmentation or complete separation of the segments.

Looped cords are relatively thin and fold back on themselves, sometimes more than once. Looped cords generally indicate members of the weasel family.

Tails are found on scat belonging to many carnivores and porcupines. The tails on carnivore scat taper and consist of hairs. Those on porcupine scat consist of vegetable matter and often join together two or more pellets. Connecting tails are occasionally found in scat of porcupines and beavers.

Clumps or groups of pellets are characteristic of ungulates. When the diet is moist, the separate forms of the pellets may be hard to distinguish. However, as the diet dries out, separate pellets are obvious, but the clumps still stick together When slightly drier the pellets fall apart as the clump hits the ground. In drier scat, the pellets separate as they leave the animal and form a trail on the ground.

Size and Quantity

Although size and quantity provide important clues about relative body size within families, they do not provide positive identification. The diameter, which is controlled by the maximum size of the anus, is somewhat diagnostic, but great variability still exists (see earlier discussion). Since there is no control on length, the length of scat is too variable to be a diagnostic clue. The total amount of scat enables us to estimate relative size within the bear and deer families.

Color

Distinct color variations found in scat provide clues to what the animal was eating. Black scat indicates that carnivores were feeding on a mostly pure meat diet. Darker or black scat in herbivores indicates feeding on moist vegetation. White scat indicates older scat, phosphate from chewed bones or fungus digesting the scat. Gray indicates a mixture of hair and meat. Vegetable matter colors scat brown. If you break brown scat in two, you will often find tiny bits of wood. Blue scat contains berries. Green carnivore scat, which is usually very soft, tells us the animal was eating grass.

Contents

Some materials we find in the scat may help us identify the mammals that left them. Fish scales suggest mink or otter. Crayfish parts may indicate mink or otter, but more likely the predator was a raccoon. Berries and nuts are indicative of bears. Regrettably, aluminum foil and plastic are found in scat; they tell us the mammals have been feeding on garbage.

Odor

Scat containing a large amount of animal protein has a rather strong disagreeable odor, whereas carnivore scat containing grass or especially berries may be very sweet smelling. Mustelid scat, when fresh, has a characteristic musky odor that most people can recognize. Many people believe that they can recognize the odor of fresh fox scat.

Position

Naturalist, writer, and artist Ernest Thompson Seton recognized the importance of the method and location of scat disposal in relation to the social structure and home maintained by mammals. Animals that defecate many times per day (deer defecate 20 or more times per day) cannot have one den site but must move around. Mammals that maintain one home have evolved a method of **sanitation**, including scat disposal. These mammals have longer intestines that absorb more material, allowing them to defecate only once or twice per day. Three systems of scat disposal were recognized by Seton: the **wet system**, including the use of streams; the **dry system**, including isolation and burial; and **parasitic** or **antiseptic system**, including insect and fungal decomposition. Scat disposal may also reflect a mammal's methods of communication. The location and position of scat deposition therefore relates directly to the lifestyle of mammals.

When prominently displayed, scat deposits may serve as a **territorial marking**. For instance, I have observed bears depositing scat on the scat of other animals, including domestic cows. Many different mammals may deposit scat and urine regularily at a **sign post**. These places must serve some purpose in communication that we humans cannot fully appreciate. Residents and visitors alike leave their calling cards at these sign posts. They serve as a record of who lives in the area and who has passed through.

Dogs may use forks in the trail, old carcasses, or prominent knobs as sign posts. Cats tend to bury their scat. **Burial** is more common on the hunting trail and less common near the den where the presence of scat may be serving as a territorial marking. Cats and dogs will also use mounds formed by ants as defecation points. River otters use downed logs, rocks, or prominent protrusions on the bank. Otters not only leave scat at these points but also mark with anal scent glands. The marking appears to be associated with tufts of grass. Bears, when feeding for several days on one carcass, will leave many scats around their day beds.

Rodents may use prominent scent posts that are natural in origin, constructed, or of human origin. Beavers and muskrats make **scent posts** of mud and matted grasses where they mark with anal glands. Once in a while you may find scat at these scent posts. Usually, you will find muskrat scat on logs in the water just above the water level. Beavers usually deposit their scat in the water. Other rodents tend to deposit scat on open patches of soil or bare objects such as cardboard or wood. You can use this tendency to take a census of the rodents in an area. Lay pieces of **tile** or cardboard in a grid on the ground and check them daily. By using food (grains) color-coded with **dyes**, you can delineate home ranges by mapping where colored scat occur on the tiles.

Many rodents have **latrines** where they defecate regularly. Some examples include voles, pocket gophers, kangaroo rats, and packrats. Gophers and kangaroo rats have underground rooms in their tunnels which are reserved for latrines. In the drier country of the southwest, packrat **middens** (dens) may be coated with scat and urine deposits dating back thousands of years. These deposits also include vegetation from the time of deposition. Analyses of the vegetation provides us detailed information about the climate when the scat were deposited. A section through the deposit reveals climatic change over the centuries.

Many animals use water to dispose of scat. Bobcats living near streams will deposit their scat in the water. This is also true for beavers and occasionally for raccoon.

Ungulates, especially moose and elk, tend to defecate in or very near their **day beds** immediately after rising. You may see large deposits of scat from sheep on the prominent ridges where they congregate. While grazing, ungulates are on the move, and pellets tend to be spread out in grassy areas.

Habitat

It is worth repeating the importance of the stage-setting clue—habitat—in limiting the possible identification of scat.

Photographs

We have provided four pages of color photographs to illustrate the rich details found in scat. As you read the following discussion of scat refer often to the color plates. See pages 131-134.

SCAT COMPARISONS

Dog Family

Dog family scats are thick cords and occasionally folded cords. The end of the scat that leaves the anus last has a pointed tail. When the scats are broken into several parts, only the last segment has a tail. Colors which are diet dependent include white, gray, brown, and black. Often large items are present in the scat. These include seeds, insect remains, grass, feathers, hair, teeth, and small bones. Insect remains often include beetle elytra (hardened forewings) and grasshopper legs. Pieces of vegetation may constitute small portions of each scat. These parts were probably in the stomachs of herbivores when they were eaten. When canines feed on vegetation, the whole scat is usually composed of plant material. Dogs ingest small rocks while feeding on other items.

You will detect an acrid odor associated with fresh canine scat. Many naturalists feel that the odor is stronger during the mating season. Dogs use scat and urine for territorial markings and deposit them in elevated positions. You may find scratch marks near the scat. These scratchings, which are made by the hind feet, probably help to circulate the associated odors (see Plate 6). Often several scats will be deposited at the same point over the course of several days.

Cat Family

Cat scats are broken cords with relatively short tails, or they may be semisoft. Colors include brown, white, gray, and black depending on the proportions of prey items. Portions of prey items including insect chitin (outer shell), feathers, hair, bones, and teeth may be found in scat. Berries may be prominent in the fall, and other plants may occasionally compose the main portion of the scat.

Cat scat and urine have a strong odor and are used for territorial marking. Scat is deposited on elevated points (tree stumps and rocks) near the edges of the home range and on hunting trails. Near dens, both scat and urine are deposited in shallow holes and then covered (see Plate 7). Scratch markings around the scat are made with the front feet.

Weasel Family

Weasel family scats are folded cords with long tails often at both ends. Colors include black and brown with occasional gray. A distinct mustelid odor is associated with fresh scat. The hard scat of weasels, martens, ferrets, minks, and wolverines are similar in appearance and differ mainly in size and habitat. These scats are relatively long, folded cords and are generally dark gray or black as the diet of these animals is mostly protein. Splinters of bones, hair, and feathers are often found in the scat. Mink scat may contain fish scales or parts of crayfish. If the mink has been feeding on frogs or fish, the scat may vary from soft to semi-liquid. Minks deposit scat on elevated objects such as logs or rocks. Ferret scat is mostly deposited below ground.

Fresh otter scat is black and slimy with an oily, fish-like smell. As the scat ages, it tends to disintegrate. When otters have been feeding on fish, their scat is very fragile and disintegrates easily. Scat may be deposited at sign posts or singly along the bank.

Badger scat can be confused with coyote scat. Badgers usually deposit their scat below ground. Some dens, when excavated, have contained short tunnels with many scats, while other dens did not contain any at all.

Droppings from skunks tend to have blunter ends than those from other weasels. You may find insects in the scat. Even in the winter, insects may be present in the scats because skunks dig out hibernating insects. Skunks tend to use any crack or crevice for a den, and you may find scat associated with these. Skunks also leave their scat in trails. The striped skunks make latrines.

Raccoon Family

Raccoon scats are short, thick even-diameter cords, usually with flat ends. Raccoons tend to deposit in large piles of several individual scats. Color is black to brown, reddish, or even bleached white. The scat has a characteristic granular appearance. You will see particles of food in raccoon scat. As raccoons are omnivorous, many different items may be found in their scat. The presence of fish and crayfish will help you differentiate their scat from that of other carnivores. Scat will be deposited on branches or limbs, and latrines are often used repeatedly. Single raccoon scats not in piles can be confused with that of other carnivores, so look for other clues when you suspect raccoons.

Scats of the ringtail are variable, depending on the diet of this omnivorous mammal. Scats are cords, often with tapered ends. Sometimes the end will be flat. Color is brown to bleached white. Scats are relatively long. Those composed of vegetable parts tend to break up.

I have observed coati scat only in the Murie Collection at the Teton Science School. The scats were thick cords with flat ends. Their color was brown. In general, they resembled those of raccoons and are probably quite variable, again depending on the omnivorous diet.

Bear Family

Bear scats are thick cords with blunt ends. The quantity of scat is often great, and you may see large piles. The omnivorous bears have brown, black, and blue-colored scat from eating pine nuts, animal protein, and berries respectively. Bear scat often contains insects, especially ants, termites, and bees. You may have to look hard at the scat to identify the undigested heads of these insects. Plant remains are also common, with grasses, dandelions, horsetails, and thistles being favored. Some scat containing plant material will be black. The fibrous nature of the scat and sweeter plant smell will separate these scat from those containing animal protein. In the fall, a diet of acorns produces above-average-size brown scat. From April to October, grizzlies will raid the caches of squirrels for white-bark pine nuts, and the remains will be evident in the scat. A fall diet of berries will produce soft to semi-liquid scat.

Scats greater than 2 inches (5 cm) in diameter have been considered grizzly scat. However, Herrero reported that of 140 grizzly scats measured in Banff National Park, 60 (58%) were less than 2 inches. Larger grizzlies produce larger scat. If you use the two-inch rule, you will tend to misidentify the females, who may be with their young, and young males, a very serious error.

Lagomorphs

Lagomorphs form two types of scat: the semi-soft black scat that is rich in vitamins and the normal hard scat.

Rabbit family. The hard scats of rabbits, jackrabbits, and hares are slightly flattened spheres. In softer, moist scat, one end may have a small point. Scats are deposited in small piles or just a few pellets at a time. Their color ranges from brown to brownish-green to pale green. Brown scat is produced during the winter when the diet consists mostly of browse. The greenish-colored scat reflects increased amounts of herbs and moist vegetation that is actively growing. If you break the brown pellets in two you may discover small bits of wood. Sniff them. They have a relatively sweet smell. Rabbits deposit scat at the bases of the branches on which they are browsing. They defecate before retiring,

and you may find scat with the rabbit's resting **form**, a shallow depression in the ground.

Pika family. While you may find the soft vitamin-rich scat of rabbits, you will seldom observe that produced by pikas. Hard pika scats are more spherical than those produced by the rest of the lagomorphs. The scats are brown but often associated with or covered by white, nitrogenous urine deposits. Scat is deposited at latrines or on the top of the urine-coated rocks. Pika deposition areas may be identified by the presence of bright orange, nitrogen-loving lichens. Pika latrines may be associated with the boundaries of their territories and also with their food caches, which are found near the centers of the territories.

Rodents

Rodent scats are sausage-shaped. One end may have a slight point. You will see considerable variation even in the scat from one animal. Colors include reddish-brown, yellowish-brown, brown, and black. Contents are mostly plants. You will need a microscope to ascertain the diet from the finely-chewed materials. Many rodents use latrines and will defecate on smooth surfaces such as a board.

Mouse family. Mice usually defecate in a random manner but will occasionally have latrines for repeated use. Voles usually have latrines associated with their nests. Latrines constructed by voles differ from those of mice in that piles of vole scat will form a solid mass. Voles urinate on their scat, and their highly nitrogenous urine dries and forms bonds within the scat piles. The urine on the scat will be white. Packrats (also called woodrats) also have a highly nitrogenous urine that unites with scat and preserves it. Packrat scat is relatively large. Large, black, tarry masses you may see associated with woodrat dens apparently are accumulations of the black soft type of scat.

Muskrats defecate on stream banks and on logs only slightly above water level. Their scat is dark to black and often semi-liquid. In the spring the scats are prominately displayed to delineate territories. Later in the year defecation occurs primarily in the water.

Beaver family. Beavers defecate in the water. Beaver scats can be quite large, up to an inch (2.5 cm) in diameter. The scats are composed of large chunks of wood which may be apparent on the surface. These will quickly disintegrate in the water. Scat may occasionally be found floating on the water surface.

Squirrel family. Squirrels defecate on logs and stumps. Scat may be found at their main eating places associated with **middens** (refuge heaps of conifer cone scales). Individual pellets are often irregular and some may approach spherical shapes. Squirrel pellets from a single defecation will form small clumps when the diet is moist. Winter scat are darker, almost black. During the summer, insects are found in squirrel scat.

Prairie dog scats are relatively large and vary greatly from spheres to long sausages. One end tends to taper to a short tail. Colors vary from light brown to black. The brown scat contains a larger amount of woody material. Prairie dogs deposit their scat singly or in small numbers near the entrance to their burrows. Above ground latrines don't exist. I suspect that many scats are deposited below ground, perhaps in latrine rooms.

Ground squirrel scats tend to be joined by tails. A few scat will be found around the entrances to the burrows. Perhaps other scat are deposited below ground. Chipmunks deposit their scat at random.

Marmot scats exhibit great variability, ranging from sausage-shaped pellets to folded cords. The color is usually black. Deposition is at latrine sites near their burrow entrances or observation rocks. Large quantities of scat is present in these latrines.

Porcupine family. Porcupine scats are woody and tails occur frequently. Tails may join two or more scats into strings. Yellow and red scats are produced during the winter when the diet consists of greater than 70% conifers. The larger the amount of conifers, the redder the color. Black pellets are produced when porcupines feed mostly on the ground during the summer. The pellets consist of grasses, herbs, and shrubs. You may find large quantities of scat at the base of trees that porcupines have used for several days or at dens they have used in the winter.

Pocket gopher family. Gopher scats look like blunt-ended sausages. Color is usually brown. You probably won't find them during the summer since defecation occurs below ground. In the spring when snow melt reveals winter nests, you may find scats in large quantities. The scat will be scattered through the nests and the plant material packed into snow passages.

Pocket mouse family. The scat of pocket mice and kangaroo rats varies from dark green to black. It is deposited in burrows underground. Little information has been recorded about the scat of this interesting rodent family.

Ungulates

Variability in shape and color often makes it impossible for us to identify scat to the species that dropped it. The shape of ungulate scat varies considerably with moisture content; dry diets produce separate pellets, and moist diets produce semi-liquid clumps that resemble "cow-pies." Increasing moisture in the diet causes the pellets of a clump to coalesce. Pellets from drier diets exhibit a relatively large sausage shape. There is a tendency for the scat to resemble candy kisses in shape. Earlier I described the nipple-dimple pellet shape; the best example is elk scat.

Ungulates deposit pellets in large clumps or groups. Color varies from brown for drier and coarser plant material to black for moist herbaceous material. You will notice a definite ungulate odor associated with the scat and urine; it is particularly prominent during the rutting season in the fall. Often relative size is the best distinguishing factor among species.

Deer family. Deer pellets are highly variable, but drier ones tend to be blunt on one end and have a small point at the other end. Pellets may be ¾-inch (2 cm) long. Occasionally, striations may run the length of each pellet. Elk pellets show a depression or dimple at one end and a nipple at the other end. Summer elk pellets are dark but tend to become more brown as they age. Moose pellets are rounded at both ends. I believe that the rounding at both ends of pellets is the result of a very dry, coarse, woody diet. In Canyonlands, I have collected deer pellets that were rounded at both ends and merely a miniature version of moose pellets found in Yellowstone. Elk feeding on a dry woody diet also produce pellets rounded at both ends. The outside of the deer, elk, and moose pellets does not show the composition of the diet. However, if you break the pellets open, you will see plant formation.

Pronghorn antelope family. Pellets tend to be teardrop-shaped, with one end blunt and the other pointed. The sides of pronghorn pellets are less parallel than those of the deer family. Many pellet groups have elongated pellets, which have a definite point at one end. As moisture content increases, pellets coalesce into large clumps. Often when these clumps hit the ground, they will flatten on one side. Pronghorn pellets may be hard to tell from sheep pellets where the two species occur together. I have noticed that there is a greater tendency for antelope scat to become covered with white fungus than for that of the other ungulates.

Bison and sheep family. For a large part of the year, bison or buffalo tend to leave large, up to a foot long (30 cm), semi-soft patties known as **chips**. On dry feed, bison produce a layered scat with each layer stacked directly on top of the previous one. Young bison seem to leave the layered scat more than adults do. The small scat of younger bison is confusing; it is smaller than you would expect for scat coming from so large a mammal. Color is generally brown. The large scats of bison burn well when they are dried. Pioneers on the great plains used **"buffalo chips"** as their sole source of fuel for fires.

In Greenland, I found muskox scat to be of the dry pellet type. The moist, cow-pie type was not common. This may be because muskox must feed on dry low tundra vegetation. Muskoxen feeding on lush grass will probably produce more semi-soft scat. The color is brown.

Sheep scat shows great variability and can be very hard to tell from antelope scat where the two mammals occur together. Drier pellets tend to be elongated and rounded at both ends, although many will have a point at one end. Dry sheep pellets have a greater tendency to approach a spherical shape than do antelope pellets. In moister scat, pellets may be concave on one side and you will find clumps consisting of a few pellets. Individual pellets are hard to distinguish. Color varies from brown to black.

Mountain goat scat may be confused with sheep and deer scat, but individual pellets tend to be smaller. In the moist type, I believe that pellets may show a greater tendency towards layering. Color is brown to black.

Bibliography

Adams, L., G. O'Regan, and D.J. Dunaway. 1962. Analysis of forage consumption by fecal examination. J. Wildl. Mgmt., 26:108-111.

Bang, P., and P. Dahlstrom. 1974. Collins guide to animal tracks and signs. Collins, St. James Place, London. 240 pp.

Brown, T., and B. Morgan. 1983. Tom Brown's field guide to nature observation and tracking. Berkley Books, New York, 282 pp.

Bullock, R.E. 1974. Functional analysis of locomotion in pronghorn antelope. Pp. 274-305 in V. Geist and F. Walther (eds). Symposium on the Behavior of Ungulates and Its Relations to Management. Publ. Int. Union Conserv. Nat. Resour., New Ser., 24.

Casey, D. 1985. Black-footed ferret. Dodd, Mead & Company, New York, 64 pp.

Chapman, J.A., and G.A. Feldhamer, eds. 1982. Wild mammals of North America: biology, management, and economics. Johns Hopkins University Press. Baltimore, 1147 pp.

Cox, G. 1975. Winter signs in the snow. Michael Kesend Publishing, Ltd., New York, 80 pp.

Danner, D.A., and N. Dodd. 1982. Comparison of coyote and gray fox scat diameters. J. Wildl. Mgmt., 46:240-241.

DeBlase, A.F., and R.E. Martin. 1974. A manual of mammalogy. Wm. C. Brown Company Publishers, Dubuque, Iowa, 329 pp.

Eisenberg, J.F. 1981. The mammalian radiations: an analysis of trends in evolution, adaptation, and behavior. University of Chicago Press, Chicago, 610 pp.

Ewer, R.F. 1973. The carnivores. Cornell University Press, Ithaca, New York, 494 pp.

Green, J.S., and J.T. Flinders. 1981. Diameter and pH comparisons of coyote and red fox scats. J. Wildl. Mgmt., 45:765-767.

Halfpenny, J.C. 1986. A naturalist's field book. A Naturalist's World, Box 8005, Suite 357, Boulder, CO. 80306-8005. 111 pp.

Hall, R.R. 1981. The mammals of North America. John Wiley and Sons, New York, 1265 pp.

Headstrom, R. 1971. Identifying animal tracks: mammals, birds and other animals of the Eastern United States. Dover Publications, Inc., New York, 141 pp.

Herman, S.G. 1980. The naturalist's field journal. A manual of instruction based on a system established by Joseph Grinnell. Buteo Books, Vermillion, SD, 200 pp.

Herrero, S. 1985. Bear attacks: their causes and avoidance. Nick Lyon Books, Winchester Press, Piscataway, NJ, 287 pp.

Hildebrand, M. 1959. Motions of the running cheetah and horse. J. Mamm., 40:481-495.

Hildebrand, M. 1961. Further studies on locomotion of the cheetah. J. Mamm., 42:84-91.

Hildebrand, M. 1965. Symmetrical gaits of horses. Science, 150:701-709.

Hildebrand, M. 1977. Analysis of asymmetrical gaits. J. Mamm., 58:131-156.

Holechek, J.L., B. Gross, S.M. Dabo, and T. Stephenson. 1982. Effects of sample preparation, growth stage, and observer on microhistological analysis of herbivore diets. J. Wildl. Mgmt., 46:502-505.

Howell, A.B. 1944. Speed in animals. University of Chicago Press, Chicago, 270 pp.

Johnson, M.K., and D.R. Aldred. 1982. Mammalian prey digestibility by bobcats. J. Wildl. Mgmt., 46:530.

Johnson, M.K., and A.B. Carey. 1979. Porcupine pellet pH, color, and composition. Southwestern Nat., 24:554-555.

Johnson, M.K., and R.M. Hansen. 1977. Comparison of point frame and hand separation of coyote scats. J. Wildl. Mgmt., 41:319-320.

Johnson, M.K., and R.M. Hansen. 1978. Estimating dry weights per occurrence for taxa in coyote scats. J. Wildl. Mgmt., 42:913-915.

Johnson, M.K., D.R. Aldred, and T.E. Martin. 1981. Feces, bile acids and furbearers. 1143-1150 in J. Chapman and D. Purseley (eds). Intl. Assoc. Fish and Wildl. Agencies, Washington, D.C. Worldwide Furbearer Conference Proceedings. 3 Vols. 2056 pp.

Johnson, M.K., R.C. Belden, and D.R. Aldred. 1984. Differentiating mountain lion and bobcat scats. J. Wildl. Mgmt., 48:239-244.

Major, M., M.K. Johnson, W.S. Davis, and T.F. Kellogg. 1980. Identifying scats by recovery of bile acids. J. Wildl. Mgmt., 44:290-293.

Miller, D. 1981. Track finder. A guide to mammal tracks of eastern North America. Nature Study Guild. Berkeley, CA, 61 pp.

Murie, A. 1981. The grizzlies of Mt. McKinley. Nat. Park Ser., Spec. Mono. Ser., 14:1-251.

Murie, O.J. 1954. A field guide to animal tracks. Houghton Mifflin Company, Boston, 376 pp.

Muybridge, E. 1957. Animals in motion. Dover Publication, Inc., New York, 72 pp. + 183 plates.

Nagy, J.G., and J.G. Gilbert. 1968. Fecal pH values of mule deer and grazing domestic sheep. J. Wildl. Mgmt., 32:961-962.

Ormond, C. 1975. How to track and find game. Outdoor Life Books, Funk & Wagnalls, New York, 152 pp.

Rollins, D., F.C. Bryant, and R. Montandon. 1984. Fecal pH and defecation rates of eight ruminants fed known diets. J. Wildl. Mgmt., 48:807-813.

Rue, L.L., III. 1968. Sportsman's guide to game animals. Outdoor Life Books, Harper & Row, New York, 655 pp.

Schemnitz, S.D., ed. 1980. Wildlife management techniques manual. Wildlife Society, Washington, D.C., 686 pp.

Scribner, K.T., R.J. Warren, and S.L. Beasom. 1984. Eletrophoretic identification of white-tailed and mule deer feces: a preliminary assessment. J. Wildl. Mgmt., 48:656-658.

Seton, E.T. 1925. On the study of scatology. J. Mamm. 6:47-49.

Seton, E.T. 1958. Animal tracks and hunter signs. Macmillan of Canada, Toronto, 160 pp.

Shea, D.S. 1969. Animal tracks of Glacier National Park. Glacier National History Association, Kalispell, MT, 42 pp.

Smith, R.P. 1982. Animal tracks and signs of North America. Stackpole Books, Harrisburg, Pennsylvania, 271 pp.

Stackpole Books. 1958. Guide to Animal Tracks. Stackpole Books, Harrisburg, Pennsylvania, 96 pp.

Turkowski, F.J. 1980. Carnivore food habits and habitat use in ponderosa pine forests. USDA Forest Service, Research Paper, RM-215:1-9.

Vaughan, T.A. 1972. Mammalogy. W.B. Saunders Company, Philadelphia, 463 pp.

Voth, E.H., and H.C. Black. 1973. A histological technique for determining feeding habits of small herbivores. J. Wildl. Mgmt., 37:223-231.

Weaver, J.L., and S.H. Fritts. 1979. Comparison of coyote and wolf scat diameters. J. Wildl. Mgmt., 43:786-788.

Weaver, J.L., and S.W. Hoffman. 1979. Differential detectability of rodents in coyote scats. J. Wildl. Mgmt., 43:783-786.

Index

Mammal	Date	Length	Width	Stride	Straddle	Group	Inter-group
Domestic Dog							
Foxes							
Kit							
Swift							
Red							
Gray							
Arctic							
Coyote							
Wolf							
Domestic cat							
Margay cat							
Jaguarundi cat							
Bobcat							
Ocelot							
Lynx							
Lion							
Jaguar							
Pikas							
Rocky Mountain							
Collard							
Cottontails							
Mountain							
Desert							
Eastern							
New England							
Jackrabbit							
Antelope							
White-tailed							
Black-tailed							

Mammal	Date	Length	Width	Stride	Straddle	Group	Inter-group
Hares							
Arctic							
Snowshoe							
Tundra							
Mountain beaver							
Squirrels							
Ground							
Arctic							
Franklin's							
Richardson's							
Thirteen-lined							
Golden mantled							
other							
Tree							
Abert's							
Chickaree (red)							
Fox							
Grey							
Flying							
Chipmunks							
Easter							
Least							
Other							
Prairie Dog							
Beaver							
Pocket gophers							
Thomomys							
Geomys							
Cratogeomys							

Mammal	Date	Length	Width	Stride	Straddle	Group	Inter-group
Kangaroo rats							
Mice							
Pocket							
Harvest							
Jumping							
Deer (White-footed)							
Grasshopper							
Rats							
Woodrats							
Packrat							
Muskrat							
Rice Rat							
Cotton rat							
Water rat							
Voles							
Microtus							
Phenacomys							
Red back							
Sage brush							
Lemmings							
Bog							
Brown							
Collared							
Porcupine							
Old World							
Mouse							
Rat							

Mammal	Date	Length	Width	Stride	Straddle	Group	Inter-group
Bears							
Black							
Grizzly							
Polar							
Weasels							
Leaset							
Short-tailed							
Long-tailed							
Ferrets							
Black-footed							
Domestic							
Mink							
Marten							
Fisher							
Wolverine							
Badger							
Skunks							
Striped							
Spotted							
Hog-nosed							
Hooded							
Otter							
River							
Sea							
Raccoon							
Coati							
Ringtail							
Oppossum							
Shrews							

Mammal	Date	Length	Width	Stride	Straddle	Group	Inter-group
Moles							
Peccary							
Deer							
White-tailed							
Mule							
Elk							
Moose							
Caribou							
Antelope							
Bison							
Muskox							
Mountain Goat							
Sheep							
Bighorn							
Dall							
Bats							
Humans							
Armadillo							
Other Domestic Mammals							
European Hare							
Goat							
Pig							
Wild Boar							
Cow							
Horse							
Donkey							

SCAT COMPARISON KEY

OUTLINE DRAWING	SHAPE	NUMBER	COLOR	TROPHIC LEVEL
	SPHERE (slightly flattened)	Few and scattered	Brownish-green Pale green	Herbivores
	ELONGATE SPHERE (large)	Clumps or groups and scattered	Brown Black	Herbivores
	ELONGATE SPHERE (small)	Few or in latrines	Reddish-brown Brown Black	Herbivores
	ELONGATE SPHERE (small)	Few	Black Brown	Carnivores
	THICK CORD	Single or several at a scent post	White Grey Brown Black	Carnivores
	THICK CORDS	Single or large piles	Brown Black Blue	Omnivores
	THICK CORDS	Single or piles	Black Brown Red White	Omnivores
	LOOPED CORDS	Single	Black Brown Dark Grey	Carnivores to Omnivores
	BROKEN CORDS	Single	Brown Black Gray White	Carnivores
	Non-descript	Single	Brown Black	Omnivore

SCAT COMPARISON KEY

SCAT TYPES	NOTES	GROUP	PAGE NUMBER
Soft and Hard	Finely chewed material	Lagomorph Order	146
Hard	Nipple-dimple shape Stacks of pellets Moist "chips" or "pies"	Deer Order	147
Soft and Hard	Finely chewed materials From very small to one inch (2.5 cm) in diameter	Rodent Order	146
Hard	Very small scat which is similar to mouse	Shrew Order	- - -
Hard	Single pointed end Hair and bones Occasional plant material	Dog Family	144
Hare	Blunt ends Insect and berries Hair and bones	Bear Family	145
Hard	Flat to tapered ends Often granular	Raccoon Family	145
Hard	Mustelid odor Hair and few bones Pointed to blunt ends	Weasel Family	145
Hard	Segmented, especially if dry environment Often buried Hair, bones, vegetation	Cat Family	144
Hard	Varies considerably with diet, seldom solid	Opossum Family	- - -